CAREER EXAMINATION SERIES

THIS IS YOUR **PASSBOOK**® FOR ...

ACCOUNT CLERK

NLC®

NATIONAL LEARNING CORPORATION®
passbooks.com

COPYRIGHT NOTICE

Copyright © 2021 by

NLC®

National Learning Corporation

212 Michael Drive, Syosset, NY 11791
(516) 921-8888 • www.passbooks.com
E-mail: info@passbooks.com

PUBLISHED IN THE UNITED STATES OF AMERICA

PASSBOOK® SERIES

THE *PASSBOOK® SERIES* has been created to prepare applicants and candidates for the ultimate academic battlefield – the examination room.

At some time in our lives, each and every one of us may be required to take an examination – for validation, matriculation, admission, qualification, registration, certification, or licensure.

Based on the assumption that every applicant or candidate has met the basic formal educational standards, has taken the required number of courses, and read the necessary texts, the *PASSBOOK® SERIES* furnishes the one special preparation which may assure passing with confidence, instead of failing with insecurity. Examination questions – together with answers – are furnished as the basic vehicle for study so that the mysteries of the examination and its compounding difficulties may be eliminated or diminished by a sure method.

This book is meant to help you pass your examination provided that you qualify and are serious in your objective.

The entire field is reviewed through the huge store of content information which is succinctly presented through a provocative and challenging approach – the question-and-answer method.

A climate of success is established by furnishing the correct answers at the end of each test.

You soon learn to recognize types of questions, forms of questions, and patterns of questioning. You may even begin to anticipate expected outcomes.

You perceive that many questions are repeated or adapted so that you can gain acute insights, which may enable you to score many sure points.

You learn how to confront new questions, or types of questions, and to attack them confidently and work out the correct answers.

You note objectives and emphases, and recognize pitfalls and dangers, so that you may make positive educational adjustments.

Moreover, you are kept fully informed in relation to new concepts, methods, practices, and directions in the field.

You discover that you arre actually taking the examination all the time: you are preparing for the examination by "taking" an examination, not by reading extraneous and/or supererogatory textbooks.

In short, this PASSBOOK®, used directedly, should be an important factor in helping you to pass your test.

ACCOUNT CLERK

DUTIES:

The work involves performing specialized clerical work in keeping financial records of some variety and complexity. Using a single or double entry system, an employee in this class keeps books or records subject to audit. Duties may include utilization of computers or word processors with financial capabilities. The work is performed in accordance with clearly established accounting methods and procedures and is reviewed primarily through verification of financial records and statements. The employee in this class receives remittances by mail or in person; verifies amount, computes interest and penalties and posts to book or original entry; assists in maintaining labor, material and operational cost records; issues receipts for monies received; classifies constantly recurring receipts and expenditures and distributes costs according to prescribed code; and operates computing, calculating, check writing and other office machines. Supervision may be exercised over a small number of subordinate clerical personnel. Does related work as required.

EXAMPLES OF WORK:

Reviews a variety of documents such as claim forms, vouchers, bills, purchase orders, to determine eligibility for payment or to verify accuracy of payment made, according to defined procedures and policies; verifies all calculations and codes on documents; posts figures to appropriate accounts either manually or through a computer, verifying all data entered; reconciles all entries, both debits and credits; prepares simple financial or statistical reports from data entered, including status of accounts, current balances, cash received or paid; produces data needed for state and federal reimbursement claims; receives cash payments, issues receipts; prepares checks for disbursement, deposits funds into appropriate accounts, prepares reconciliation of balances and posts balances to appropriate ledgers; makes bank deposits as necessary; contacts clients, vendors, etc., to obtain additional information as necessary; provides routine information orally or in writing in response to inquiries on financial records; files and maintains all related records such as records related to processing of payrolls, invoices, vouchers, bills, correspondence; receives, balances, audits, and prepares payroll time records; processes data either for computer or other records; makes computations as necessary; operates calculator, computer terminal, printer and other related office equipment.

SCOPE OF THE EXAMINATION

The written test will cover knowledge, skills and/or abilities in such areas as:

1. **Clerical operations with letters and numbers** - These questions test your skills and abilities in clerical operations involving alphabetizing, comparing, checking and counting. The questions require you to follow the specific directions given for each question which may involve alphabetizing, comparing, checking and counting given groups of letters and/or numbers.

2. **Arithmetic computation** - These questions test your ability to do addition, subtraction, multiplication, and division. Questions may also involve fractions, decimals, averages, and percents.

3. **Arithmetic reasoning** - These questions test your ability to solve an arithmetic problem presented in sentence or short paragraph form. You must read the problem, understand the situation presented, decide what must be done to solve it, and apply the appropriate arithmetic operation(s) in the appropriate order in order to determine the correct solution. Knowledge of addition, subtraction, multiplication, and division is necessary. Questions may also involve the use of percents, decimals, and fractions.

HOW TO PREPARE GUIDE FOR

ACCOUNT CLERK

WRITTEN EXAMINATION

I.   INTRODUCTION

The purpose of these instructions is to help you prepare for the written, entry-level qualifying examination which is being given for the Account Clerk classification. The Account Clerk Qualifying Exam is the exam you are taking in order to be hired as an Account Clerk.

It is very important that you sit down in a quiet place and review the material in this booklet. You should also set aside time to practice doing the things that are suggested in this booklet to prepare for the Qualifying Exam. Please remember that the material in this booklet is designed to help you prepare for the exam. You will not need the material in this booklet at the time you actually take the exam. Therefore, you will not be allowed to carry this booklet into the exam session. Later in this booklet, we will instruct you on what you are allowed to bring to the exam session and what you **must** bring to the exam session. You will not be allowed to bring this booklet to the exam with you.

II.   JOB PREVIEW

Account Clerks are responsible for the performance of moderately difficult clerical accounting functions. Work at this level contrasts with the routine record keeping tasks assigned other clerical positions by the addition of difficult and responsible accounting-related clerical duties. As incumbents gain experience, more complex accounting duties are assigned. Work requires use of some judgment and interpretation of departmental and fiscal policies and regulations and consideration of alternatives. Employees make decisions based on applicable functions, rules, and regulations of the organization and solve problems identified by others. Work is reviewed to determine compliance with established rules, regulations, and procedures and may also involve technical guidance and minor supervision over clerical employees.

III.   PREPARING FOR THE EXAM

A.   General Information on What to do Before the Exam

Here are some suggestions for what to do before the exam and for getting to the testing location on time and with the proper things that you will need to take the test.

- Be well rested. Get a good night's sleep for several nights in a row before the written exam.

- Allow plenty of time to get to the exam site. If you are rushed and late, you may be upset when you get there. Plan to arrive at least 20 minutes before the exam start time.

- Do not bring a cell phone to the testing site. Pagers should only be brought if it is absolutely necessary. All pagers must be set to the vibration mode.

- Come dress comfortably. The total time provided for completion of the exam will be three hours.

- You should read and study this booklet. You should practice the kind of things that this booklet suggests that you practice.

- Do **not** bring this or any other booklets, reading, or study materials to the exam. You **will not** be permitted to bring them in. All materials needed to complete the exam will be given to you at the exam.

- You **must** bring the Exam Notification Letter or Notification Postcard that you received from the Personnel Department to the examination site.

- To protect your own interests, you will also be asked to bring Picture Identification to the examination site. This may be a valid driver's license, a military identification card, a student identification card, or some other form of Picture Identification. You only need one form of Picture Identification.

- You **will not be allowed** to enter the examination site or take the exam without your Notification Letter/Postcard **and** Picture Identification.

- Bring several number 2 pencils with erasers to the exam. It is also recommended that you bring a highlighter pen and a calculator. You may bring a calculator to use for the examination. Small solar powered or battery operated calculators that perform basic functions such as addition, subtraction, multiplication, division, square roots, or percentages are allowed. Calculators that plug in, utilize tape, have word processing, spelling, thesauruses, or other storage and retrieval capabilities (except basic memory functions) are not allowed. **Calculators that are a feature on a cell phone are not permitted.** Calculators are subject to inspection by exam monitors. Applicants may not borrow or share calculators at the exam site.

B. General Information on What to do During the Examination

Some people are nervous when they take tests. There is nothing wrong with that. Whenever you are going to do something important, it is good to feel a bit keyed-up. It is nature's way of getting you warmed up and ready, like an actress or actor about to go on stage for a performance. However, it is not good to be so nervous that all you can think about is how nervous you are. You need to keep your mind on the test questions, and not on your feelings. To improve your ability to do that, you will find ideas in this booklet on how to study and prepare for the written exam. **The more**

prepared you are, the more comfortable and less nervous you will feel during the exam.

- In an exam like this one, some questions are easy and some are hard. Don't give up. Probably no one will make a perfect score. If it is hard for you to figure out an answer, it is probably hard for other people too. Keep your mind on the test, and try to answer every question. Mark an answer on your answer sheet even if it is a guess. **You will not be penalized for guessing.** On the other hand, do not spend too much time on any one question just because it is hard. This may not leave you enough time to answer questions that you know.

- You will have three hours to complete the exam. Use your time efficiently. The exam is not a test of how quickly you can answer the questions. However, it does not allow you all the time you might like to have. In the parts of the test that require reading, try to keep a steady pace. Try to finish as much of the test as you can.

- An examination monitor will be at your test site when you report. The monitor will check your Picture Identification and Exam Notification Letter/Postcard, and then will provide you with test materials. You **must** follow the instructions of the monitor at all times.

- The examination monitor will provide you with instructions concerning restroom availability during the test administration. It is important to remember that the time that you take to use the restroom is time away from working on the examination. So, we recommend that you use the restroom before the examination, if possible.

- You are not to open the examination booklets or instructions or begin working on the exam until you are instructed by the monitor to do so.

- The only materials you need to bring to the test site are a Picture Identification, Exam Notification Letter/Postcard, several number 2 pencils. You may bring a calculator to use for the Account Clerk examination. Small solar powered or battery operated calculators that perform basic functions such as addition, subtraction, multiplication, division, square roots, or percentages are allowed. Calculators that plug in, utilize tape, have word processing, spelling, thesauruses, or other storage and retrieval capabilities (except basic memory functions) are not allowed. **Calculators that are a feature on a cell phone are not permitted.** Calculators are subject to inspection by exam monitors. Applicants may not borrow or share calculators at the exam site. No other materials will be allowed in the test site.

- Candidates making any disturbances or caught cheating will be disqualified from the exam.

- Test monitors can answer questions concerning exam administration issues only. They **will not** be able to interpret exam questions for you.

- You should always check to make sure that your answers to questions are marked in the location on the answer sheet that matches the number of the question you are answering.

- If you have time remaining after you have completed the test, it is always a good idea to review your responses on the more difficult questions. Once you have finished, notify the monitor for instructions.

In summary, there are two things you can do that make you feel more comfortable taking the exam: (1) follow the guidelines presented in this booklet on how to prepare for the exam, and (2) become familiar with the kinds of questions that will be used in the exam.

IV. EXAM INFORMATION

A. General Exam Information

A study of the Account Clerk classification was conducted prior to developing the examination. A number of employees who work in this position and their supervisors participated in this study. The study showed that the following knowledges and abilities are associated with the above duties. These knowledges and abilities are needed on the first day of work before training.

- **Knowledge of bookkeeping such as reconciliations, journal entries, journal vouchers, debits, credits, accounts payable, and accounts receivable as needed to check invoices for accuracy, process vouchers, record financial transactions, and make corrections to financial records.**

- **Knowledge of accounting terminology such as debits, credits, general ledgers, warrants, and journal vouchers as needed to communicate with accounting personnel/vendors and document financial transactions.**

- **Knowledge of filing systems such as alphanumeric, alphabetical, chronological, etc. as needed to ensure easy retrieval and meet record retention requirements.**

- Ability to operate a computer as needed to access/retrieve/store information, prepare letters, memos, etc., enter data, generate reports, prepare spreadsheets, process payment transactions, and provide/receive information through email.

- **Ability to read and comprehend narrative information such as correspondence, departmental manuals, contracts, bids, bid specifications, state and federal regulations, and catalogs as needed to ensure compliance with rules and regulations, provide requested information, and remain current on departmental procedures and requirements.**

- **Ability to perform basic math to include adding, subtraction, multiplication, division, percentages as needed to verify invoices,**

calculate costs, calculate leave balances, conduct inventory, determine refunds, order supplies, provide budget estimates, balance purchase orders, and prepare requisitions.

- Ability to operate office equipment such as copier, fax, printer, scanner, telephone, calculator, cash register and shredder as needed to maximize work time, receive and transmit information, and store and analyze information.

- Ability to follow oral and written instructions as needed to accomplish assigned tasks and responsibilities and comply with appropriate policies and procedures.

- Ability to communicate orally to vendors, general public, co-workers, other state agencies, and supervisor as needed to answer questions, provide/obtain information/instructions, request assistance, and resolve discrepancies.

- **Ability to pay close attention to detail as needed to verify invoices and ensure proper completion of documents.**

- Ability to establish and maintain effective working relationships with vendors, co-workers, other state agencies, general public, and supervisor as needed to achieve departmental/agency goals, promote teamwork, and maximize goods and services.

- Ability to be flexible as needed to accomplish assigned work and perform additional duties in absence of co-workers or as needed.

- Ability to work on multiple tasks simultaneously as needed to meet deadlines and ensure required tasks are accomplished.

- Ability to plan and organize to include time management and prioritizing tasks as needed to meet deadlines and achieve objectives.

- Ability to maintain confidentiality as needed to ensure employee/client privacy and comply with department/state/federal requirements.

- **Ability to compose correspondence such as letters, memos, and reports to include utilizing proper sentence structured, grammar, punctuation, and spelling as needed to provide/request information, respond to inquiries, obtain equipment and supplies, and maintain documentation for auditing purposes.**

- **Ability to file documents such as employee records, purchase orders, requisitions, vouchers, and inventory records as needed to retrieve in a timely manner, maintain documentation, and ensure accessibility for future reference.**

- **Ability to compare information such as invoices to shipping tickets, requisitions to purchase orders, and leave slips to leave reports as**

needed to identify/correct errors, and ensure balance.

- Ability to maintain accurate records as needed to ensure appropriate documentation and meet documentation requirements.

- **Ability to proof documents as needed to verify accuracy and identify errors.**

- Ability to work independently with minimal supervision as needed to perform assigned tasks and meet required deadlines.

The examination for Account Clerk will measure the knowledges and abilities above that appear in **bold print**. The remaining knowledges and abilities must be demonstrated during the probationary period if you are hired into an Account Clerk position.

V. ADDITIONAL INFORMATION FOR TAKING THIS EXAM

A.   Effective Note Taking

Why Take Notes?

There are several good reasons to take notes:

- Taking notes can help you remember; notes you take in your own words are easier to understand and remember.

- Writing down notes may actually make ideas you did not fully understand clearer.

Taking Effective Notes

The following are some rules and suggestions for taking effective notes:

- Make your notes brief. Pick out the important points.

- Do not use a sentence when you can use a phrase. Do not use a phrase when you can use a word.

- Use abbreviations whenever possible.

- Put most notes in your own words. However, copy the following exactly as they are presented:

  a.   Definitionsd
  b.   Specific Facts
  c.   Specific Rules and Procedures

B.   Strategies For Taking the Exam

By following the suggestions listed below, you can do your best:

- Read the questions carefully. Be sure you know what the question asks and what the choices say before you try to answer the question. On every test, people choose wrong answers simply because they failed to pay attention to part of the question or failed to read all of the answer.

- Choose the answer that is generally best. To keep questions short, they cannot have a lot of detail. You should give the answer that would be considered to be generally the best.

- For "Reading Comprehension" questions, decide something about each question.

  1.   You may decide you know the answer. Mark your answer on the answer sheet. Spend no more time on that question.

  2.   You may decide you are fairly sure of the answer, but may want to think more about it. Mark your answer sheet and make a note of it in the test booklet so it will be easier to find later.

  3.   You may decide one or two answers are definitely not the best. Eliminate the answers you know are wrong then direct your attention to those choices that are potentially correct.

  4.   You may decide that figuring out the answer is possible, but will take you a lot of time. Don't mark any answer. Note the question in your test booklet so you can find it when you are ready to come back to it. Make sure you finish the test in enough time to come back to answer the question.

  5.   You may decide you don't know the answer and that all you can do is make a guess. Make the guess. Mark the answer sheet to show your answer. Don't waste any more time on that question. There is no penalty for guessing and sometimes you may guess right.

- Don't change answers unless you have a good reason. When people change their answers, they more often change from a right answer to a wrong one rather than from a wrong answer to a right one. The reason seems to be that they start thinking about some specific case, which results in choosing an answer on the basis of facts that are not given in the question. Or, people think about what some part of a question says and forget about what the rest of the question said.

- Use your time efficiently. You may not have all of the time you might like to complete the test. In the parts of the test that require reading, read at a normal pace so that you can finish the test and have time to go back and work on the questions you saved until last.

- Don't give up. Many people give up too easily on test questions. If the question looks too hard, they don't even try. Look for the specific information needed to answer the question. However, do not spend too much time on any one question just because it is hard. Doing that may not leave you enough time to give the answers that you know.

C. Study Suggestions

You may find some of the following ideas helpful in preparing for the exam:

- Do not prepare for the exam in a single session.

- Study in a quiet place. Do not study when you are doing something else.

- Make up your own tests and take them.

- Pretend that you are in a real testing situation and try not to <u>talk</u> to anyone else while you are taking the sample tests.

- Practice following instructions. Read sections of how-to books or instruction manuals you may have at home and practice taking notes or highlighting important aspects of the sections.

- Study the sample test items in this booklet.

- Study whatever material you believe will assist you in learning each of the duties, and knowledges, skills, and abilities required for the Account Clerk position.

VI. EXAM ADMINISTRATION INFORMATION

A. What to Bring to the Examination

- Do **not** bring this booklet to the exam location. You will not be permitted to bring it in the testing room.

- Do **not** bring any of your study materials to the exam. This includes notes, manuals, and other study materials.

- Remember to bring to the exam the Notification Letter/Postcard that you received from the Personnel Department. You will **not be allowed** to take the exam without your Notification Letter/Postcard.

- To protect your own interests, you will also be asked to bring a Picture Identification to the exam location. This might be a valid driver's license, a military identification card, a student identification card, or some form of picture identification. You only need one form of Picture Identification.

- Bring several number 2 pencils with erasers to the exam. It is also recommended that you bring a highliter pen and a calculator.

- Remember, you will **not be allowed** to enter the exam location or take the exam without your Notification Letter/Postcard **and** Picture Identification.

B. Taking the Exam

You will be given three hours to complete the exam. Use your time efficiently. The exam is not a test of how quickly you can answer questions. However, it does not allow you the time you might like to have. In the parts of the test that require reading, try to keep a steady pace. Try to finish as much of the test as you can.

While reading passages, you may want to take a few notes. Make your notes brief. You may also want to underline or highlight important information as you read.

Don't give up. Many people give up too easily on tests. If the question or problem seems hard, they do not even try. Mark an answer on your answer sheet even if it is a guess. You will not be penalized for guessing. On the other hand, do not spend too much time on any one question just because it is hard. This may not leave you enough time to answer questions that you know.

VII. EXAMINATION DESCRIPTION

The Qualifying Examination will last three hours. When you read the word "exam" in the rest of these Instructions and Notes, it is a short way of referring to the entire Qualifying Examination.

You will find examples of exam items below. Please review these items in order to familiarize yourself with the kinds of items you will be asked and the format of the exam.

VIII. SAMPLE TEST ITEMS

The examination for Account Clerk will measure the knowledges and abilities above that appear in **bold print**. The following are examples of how your knowledge and abilities will be measured.

1. The general ledger of Company A is $360.00. The bank's statement, issued on the same day, shows bank charges of $8.00. Uncleared checks amount to $175.00 and the last deposit entered in the general ledger has not been credited by the bank. The amount of the deposit is $50.00. What is the balance on the bank statement?

   1._____

   A. $277.00   B. $427.00   C. $469.00   D. $477.00

2. Tribble, William T. would be filed between   2.____
   A. Tribble, Joseph and Tribble, Thomas
   B. Tribble, Peter and Tribble, Zachary
   C. Tribble, Walter and Tribble, Wilhelm
   D. Tribbel, W. and Tribbel, James

3. A chronological record of all transactions of a business is a(n)   3.____
   A. journal   B. chart   C. invoice   D. receipt

4. State law requires the Division of Purchasing to request sealed bids for   4.____
   purchases involving more than the minimum amount prescribed by law except
   in emergency situations or as otherwise provided by law. All bids shall be
   sealed when received and shall be opened in public. A bid not properly
   identified at bid opening will be disqualified. Bids properly identified in
   accordance with the terms and conditions of the Invitation to Bid (ITB) will be
   securely kept, unopened until the stated opening date and hour. The Division
   of Purchasing accepts no responsibility for premature opening of a bid not
   properly identified or late arrival of a bid for whatever reason. At the hour
   stated in the notice, all bids shall be opened in public for information of
   interested parties who may be present either in person or by representative.
   Such information is not to be construed as meaning any bid meets all
   specifications set out in the ITB.
   According to the preceding passage, when is the Division of Purchasing
   required to request sealed bids?
   A. Purchases over $1,000
   B. Purchases over the minimum amount set by law
   C. Emergency situations
   D. At the beginning of the fiscal year

Questions 5.

DIRECTIONS: In this section, there are questions that involve the comparison of various types
              of information. Compare the "copy" on the right against the "original" on the left
              and determine the number of errors, if any, in each set of data. Assume that
              the "original" is always correct.

ORIGINAL	COPY
Schedule for Quarterly Requisitions	Schedule of Quarterly Requisitions
January 5	January 5
April 25	April 15
July 20	July 20
October 15	October 15

5. How many errors are found in the COPY above?   5.____
   A. 0   B. 1
   C. 2   D. None of the above

6.   Select the sentence that BEST represents Standard English usage.   6._____
   A. The clerk should have known that he hadn't out to ask for supplies without a requisition.
   B. The clerk should have known that he ought not to have asked for supplies without a requisition.
   C. The clerk should have known that he should not of asked for supplies without a requisition.
   D. The clerk should of known that he ought not to ask for supplies without a requisition.

KEY (CORRECT ANSWERS)

1. D
2. B
3. A
4. B
5. C
6. B

HOW TO TAKE A TEST

I. YOU MUST PASS AN EXAMINATION

A. *WHAT EVERY CANDIDATE SHOULD KNOW*

Examination applicants often ask us for help in preparing for the written test. What can I study in advance? What kinds of questions will be asked? How will the test be given? How will the papers be graded?

As an applicant for a civil service examination, you may be wondering about some of these things. Our purpose here is to suggest effective methods of advance study and to describe civil service examinations.

Your chances for success on this examination can be increased if you know how to prepare. Those "pre-examination jitters" can be reduced if you know what to expect. You can even experience an adventure in good citizenship if you know why civil service exams are given.

B. *WHY ARE CIVIL SERVICE EXAMINATIONS GIVEN?*

Civil service examinations are important to you in two ways. As a citizen, you want public jobs filled by employees who know how to do their work. As a job seeker, you want a fair chance to compete for that job on an equal footing with other candidates. The best-known means of accomplishing this two-fold goal is the competitive examination.

Exams are widely publicized throughout the nation. They may be administered for jobs in federal, state, city, municipal, town or village governments or agencies.

Any citizen may apply, with some limitations, such as the age or residence of applicants. Your experience and education may be reviewed to see whether you meet the requirements for the particular examination. When these requirements exist, they are reasonable and applied consistently to all applicants. Thus, a competitive examination may cause you some uneasiness now, but it is your privilege and safeguard.

C. *HOW ARE CIVIL SERVICE EXAMS DEVELOPED?*

Examinations are carefully written by trained technicians who are specialists in the field known as "psychological measurement," in consultation with recognized authorities in the field of work that the test will cover. These experts recommend the subject matter areas or skills to be tested; only those knowledges or skills important to your success on the job are included. The most reliable books and source materials available are used as references. Together, the experts and technicians judge the difficulty level of the questions.

Test technicians know how to phrase questions so that the problem is clearly stated. Their ethics do not permit "trick" or "catch" questions. Questions may have been tried out on sample groups, or subjected to statistical analysis, to determine their usefulness.

Written tests are often used in combination with performance tests, ratings of training and experience, and oral interviews. All of these measures combine to form the best-known means of finding the right person for the right job.

II. HOW TO PASS THE WRITTEN TEST

A. NATURE OF THE EXAMINATION

To prepare intelligently for civil service examinations, you should know how they differ from school examinations you have taken. In school you were assigned certain definite pages to read or subjects to cover. The examination questions were quite detailed and usually emphasized memory. Civil service exams, on the other hand, try to discover your present ability to perform the duties of a position, plus your potentiality to learn these duties. In other words, a civil service exam attempts to predict how successful you will be. Questions cover such a broad area that they cannot be as minute and detailed as school exam questions.

In the public service similar kinds of work, or positions, are grouped together in one "class." This process is known as *position-classification*. All the positions in a class are paid according to the salary range for that class. One class title covers all of these positions, and they are all tested by the same examination.

B. FOUR BASIC STEPS

1) Study the announcement

How, then, can you know what subjects to study? Our best answer is: "Learn as much as possible about the class of positions for which you've applied." The exam will test the knowledge, skills and abilities needed to do the work.

Your most valuable source of information about the position you want is the official exam announcement. This announcement lists the training and experience qualifications. Check these standards and apply only if you come reasonably close to meeting them.

The brief description of the position in the examination announcement offers some clues to the subjects which will be tested. Think about the job itself. Review the duties in your mind. Can you perform them, or are there some in which you are rusty? Fill in the blank spots in your preparation.

Many jurisdictions preview the written test in the exam announcement by including a section called "Knowledge and Abilities Required," "Scope of the Examination," or some similar heading. Here you will find out specifically what fields will be tested.

2) Review your own background

Once you learn in general what the position is all about, and what you need to know to do the work, ask yourself which subjects you already know fairly well and which need improvement. You may wonder whether to concentrate on improving your strong areas or on building some background in your fields of weakness. When the announcement has specified "some knowledge" or "considerable knowledge," or has used adjectives like "beginning principles of…" or "advanced … methods," you can get a clue as to the number and difficulty of questions to be asked in any given field. More questions, and hence broader coverage, would be included for those subjects which are more important in the work. Now weigh your strengths and weaknesses against the job requirements and prepare accordingly.

3) Determine the level of the position

Another way to tell how intensively you should prepare is to understand the level of the job for which you are applying. Is it the entering level? In other words, is this the position in which beginners in a field of work are hired? Or is it an intermediate or advanced level? Sometimes this is indicated by such words as "Junior" or "Senior" in the class title. Other jurisdictions use Roman numerals to designate the level – Clerk I, Clerk II, for example. The word "Supervisor" sometimes appears in the title. If the level is not indicated by the title, check the description of duties. Will you be working under very close supervision, or will you have responsibility for independent decisions in this work?

4) Choose appropriate study materials

Now that you know the subjects to be examined and the relative amount of each subject to be covered, you can choose suitable study materials. For beginning level jobs, or even advanced ones, if you have a pronounced weakness in some aspect of your training, read a modern, standard textbook in that field. Be sure it is up to date and has general coverage. Such books are normally available at your library, and the librarian will be glad to help you locate one. For entry-level positions, questions of appropriate difficulty are chosen – neither highly advanced questions, nor those too simple. Such questions require careful thought but not advanced training.

If the position for which you are applying is technical or advanced, you will read more advanced, specialized material. If you are already familiar with the basic principles of your field, elementary textbooks would waste your time. Concentrate on advanced textbooks and technical periodicals. Think through the concepts and review difficult problems in your field.

These are all general sources. You can get more ideas on your own initiative, following these leads. For example, training manuals and publications of the government agency which employs workers in your field can be useful, particularly for technical and professional positions. A letter or visit to the government department involved may result in more specific study suggestions, and certainly will provide you with a more definite idea of the exact nature of the position you are seeking.

III. KINDS OF TESTS

Tests are used for purposes other than measuring knowledge and ability to perform specified duties. For some positions, it is equally important to test ability to make adjustments to new situations or to profit from training. In others, basic mental abilities not dependent on information are essential. Questions which test these things may not appear as pertinent to the duties of the position as those which test for knowledge and information. Yet they are often highly important parts of a fair examination. For very general questions, it is almost impossible to help you direct your study efforts. What we can do is to point out some of the more common of these general abilities needed in public service positions and describe some typical questions.

1) General information

Broad, general information has been found useful for predicting job success in some kinds of work. This is tested in a variety of ways, from vocabulary lists to questions about current events. Basic background in some field of work, such as sociology or economics, may be sampled in a group of questions. Often these are principles which have become familiar to most persons through exposure rather than through formal training. It is difficult to advise you how to study for these questions; being alert to the world around you is our best suggestion.

2) Verbal ability

An example of an ability needed in many positions is verbal or language ability. Verbal ability is, in brief, the ability to use and understand words. Vocabulary and grammar tests are typical measures of this ability. Reading comprehension or paragraph interpretation questions are common in many kinds of civil service tests. You are given a paragraph of written material and asked to find its central meaning.

3) Numerical ability

Number skills can be tested by the familiar arithmetic problem, by checking paired lists of numbers to see which are alike and which are different, or by interpreting charts and graphs. In the latter test, a graph may be printed in the test booklet which you are asked to use as the basis for answering questions.

4) Observation

A popular test for law-enforcement positions is the observation test. A picture is shown to you for several minutes, then taken away. Questions about the picture test your ability to observe both details and larger elements.

5) Following directions

In many positions in the public service, the employee must be able to carry out written instructions dependably and accurately. You may be given a chart with several columns, each column listing a variety of information. The questions require you to carry out directions involving the information given in the chart.

6) Skills and aptitudes

Performance tests effectively measure some manual skills and aptitudes. When the skill is one in which you are trained, such as typing or shorthand, you can practice. These tests are often very much like those given in business school or high school courses. For many of the other skills and aptitudes, however, no short-time preparation can be made. Skills and abilities natural to you or that you have developed throughout your lifetime are being tested.

Many of the general questions just described provide all the data needed to answer the questions and ask you to use your reasoning ability to find the answers. Your best preparation for these tests, as well as for tests of facts and ideas, is to be at your physical and mental best. You, no doubt, have your own methods of getting into an exam-taking mood and keeping "in shape." The next section lists some ideas on this subject.

IV. KINDS OF QUESTIONS

Only rarely is the "essay" question, which you answer in narrative form, used in civil service tests. Civil service tests are usually of the short-answer type. Full instructions for answering these questions will be given to you at the examination. But in case this is your first experience with short-answer questions and separate answer sheets, here is what you need to know:

1) Multiple-choice Questions

Most popular of the short-answer questions is the "multiple choice" or "best answer" question. It can be used, for example, to test for factual knowledge, ability to solve problems or judgment in meeting situations found at work.

A multiple-choice question is normally one of three types—

- It can begin with an incomplete statement followed by several possible endings. You are to find the one ending which *best* completes the statement, although some of the others may not be entirely wrong.
- It can also be a complete statement in the form of a question which is answered by choosing one of the statements listed.
- It can be in the form of a problem – again you select the best answer.

Here is an example of a multiple-choice question with a discussion which should give you some clues as to the method for choosing the right answer:

When an employee has a complaint about his assignment, the action which will *best* help him overcome his difficulty is to
A. discuss his difficulty with his coworkers
B. take the problem to the head of the organization
C. take the problem to the person who gave him the assignment
D. say nothing to anyone about his complaint

In answering this question, you should study each of the choices to find which is best. Consider choice "A" – Certainly an employee may discuss his complaint with fellow employees, but no change or improvement can result, and the complaint remains unresolved. Choice "B" is a poor choice since the head of the organization probably does not know what assignment you have been given, and taking your problem to him is known as "going over the head" of the supervisor. The supervisor, or person who made the assignment, is the person who can clarify it or correct any injustice. Choice "C" is, therefore, correct. To say nothing, as in choice "D," is unwise. Supervisors have and interest in knowing the problems employees are facing, and the employee is seeking a solution to his problem.

2) True/False Questions

The "true/false" or "right/wrong" form of question is sometimes used. Here a complete statement is given. Your job is to decide whether the statement is right or wrong.

SAMPLE: A roaming cell-phone call to a nearby city costs less than a non-roaming call to a distant city.

This statement is wrong, or false, since roaming calls are more expensive.
This is not a complete list of all possible question forms, although most of the others are variations of these common types. You will always get complete directions for

answering questions. Be sure you understand *how* to mark your answers – ask questions until you do.

V. RECORDING YOUR ANSWERS

Computer terminals are used more and more today for many different kinds of exams.

For an examination with very few applicants, you may be told to record your answers in the test booklet itself. Separate answer sheets are much more common. If this separate answer sheet is to be scored by machine – and this is often the case – it is highly important that you mark your answers correctly in order to get credit.

An electronic scoring machine is often used in civil service offices because of the speed with which papers can be scored. Machine-scored answer sheets must be marked with a pencil, which will be given to you. This pencil has a high graphite content which responds to the electronic scoring machine. As a matter of fact, stray dots may register as answers, so do not let your pencil rest on the answer sheet while you are pondering the correct answer. Also, if your pencil lead breaks or is otherwise defective, ask for another.

Since the answer sheet will be dropped in a slot in the scoring machine, be careful not to bend the corners or get the paper crumpled.

The answer sheet normally has five vertical columns of numbers, with 30 numbers to a column. These numbers correspond to the question numbers in your test booklet. After each number, going across the page are four or five pairs of dotted lines. These short dotted lines have small letters or numbers above them. The first two pairs may also have a "T" or "F" above the letters. This indicates that the first two pairs only are to be used if the questions are of the true-false type. If the questions are multiple choice, disregard the "T" and "F" and pay attention only to the small letters or numbers.

Answer your questions in the manner of the sample that follows:

32. The largest city in the United States is
  A. Washington, D.C.
  B. New York City
  C. Chicago
  D. Detroit
  E. San Francisco

1) Choose the answer you think is best. (New York City is the largest, so "B" is correct.)
2) Find the row of dotted lines numbered the same as the question you are answering. (Find row number 32)
3) Find the pair of dotted lines corresponding to the answer. (Find the pair of lines under the mark "B.")
4) Make a solid black mark between the dotted lines.

VI. BEFORE THE TEST

Common sense will help you find procedures to follow to get ready for an examination. Too many of us, however, overlook these sensible measures. Indeed, nervousness and fatigue have been found to be the most serious reasons why applicants fail to do their best on civil service tests. Here is a list of reminders:

- Begin your preparation early – Don't wait until the last minute to go scurrying around for books and materials or to find out what the position is all about.
- Prepare continuously – An hour a night for a week is better than an all-night cram session. This has been definitely established. What is more, a night a week for a month will return better dividends than crowding your study into a shorter period of time.
- Locate the place of the exam – You have been sent a notice telling you when and where to report for the examination. If the location is in a different town or otherwise unfamiliar to you, it would be well to inquire the best route and learn something about the building.
- Relax the night before the test – Allow your mind to rest. Do not study at all that night. Plan some mild recreation or diversion; then go to bed early and get a good night's sleep.
- Get up early enough to make a leisurely trip to the place for the test – This way unforeseen events, traffic snarls, unfamiliar buildings, etc. will not upset you.
- Dress comfortably – A written test is not a fashion show. You will be known by number and not by name, so wear something comfortable.
- Leave excess paraphernalia at home – Shopping bags and odd bundles will get in your way. You need bring only the items mentioned in the official notice you received; usually everything you need is provided. Do not bring reference books to the exam. They will only confuse those last minutes and be taken away from you when in the test room.
- Arrive somewhat ahead of time – If because of transportation schedules you must get there very early, bring a newspaper or magazine to take your mind off yourself while waiting.
- Locate the examination room – When you have found the proper room, you will be directed to the seat or part of the room where you will sit. Sometimes you are given a sheet of instructions to read while you are waiting. Do not fill out any forms until you are told to do so; just read them and be prepared.
- Relax and prepare to listen to the instructions
- If you have any physical problem that may keep you from doing your best, be sure to tell the test administrator. If you are sick or in poor health, you really cannot do your best on the exam. You can come back and take the test some other time.

VII. AT THE TEST

The day of the test is here and you have the test booklet in your hand. The temptation to get going is very strong. Caution! There is more to success than knowing the right answers. You must know how to identify your papers and understand variations in the type of short-answer question used in this particular examination. Follow these suggestions for maximum results from your efforts:

1) Cooperate with the monitor

The test administrator has a duty to create a situation in which you can be as much at ease as possible. He will give instructions, tell you when to begin, check to see that you are marking your answer sheet correctly, and so on. He is not there to guard you, although he will see that your competitors do not take unfair advantage. He wants to help you do your best.

2) Listen to all instructions

Don't jump the gun! Wait until you understand all directions. In most civil service tests you get more time than you need to answer the questions. So don't be in a hurry. Read each word of instructions until you clearly understand the meaning. Study the examples, listen to all announcements and follow directions. Ask questions if you do not understand what to do.

3) Identify your papers

Civil service exams are usually identified by number only. You will be assigned a number; you must not put your name on your test papers. Be sure to copy your number correctly. Since more than one exam may be given, copy your exact examination title.

4) Plan your time

Unless you are told that a test is a "speed" or "rate of work" test, speed itself is usually not important. Time enough to answer all the questions will be provided, but this does not mean that you have all day. An overall time limit has been set. Divide the total time (in minutes) by the number of questions to determine the approximate time you have for each question.

5) Do not linger over difficult questions

If you come across a difficult question, mark it with a paper clip (useful to have along) and come back to it when you have been through the booklet. One caution if you do this – be sure to skip a number on your answer sheet as well. Check often to be sure that you have not lost your place and that you are marking in the row numbered the same as the question you are answering.

6) Read the questions

Be sure you know what the question asks! Many capable people are unsuccessful because they failed to *read* the questions correctly.

7) Answer all questions

Unless you have been instructed that a penalty will be deducted for incorrect answers, it is better to guess than to omit a question.

8) Speed tests

It is often better NOT to guess on speed tests. It has been found that on timed tests people are tempted to spend the last few seconds before time is called in marking answers at random – without even reading them – in the hope of picking up a few extra points. To discourage this practice, the instructions may warn you that your score will be "corrected" for guessing. That is, a penalty will be applied. The incorrect answers will be deducted from the correct ones, or some other penalty formula will be used.

9) Review your answers

If you finish before time is called, go back to the questions you guessed or omitted to give them further thought. Review other answers if you have time.

10) Return your test materials

If you are ready to leave before others have finished or time is called, take ALL your materials to the monitor and leave quietly. Never take any test material with you. The monitor can discover whose papers are not complete, and taking a test booklet may be grounds for disqualification.

VIII. EXAMINATION TECHNIQUES

1) Read the general instructions carefully. These are usually printed on the first page of the exam booklet. As a rule, these instructions refer to the timing of the examination; the fact that you should not start work until the signal and must stop work at a signal, etc. If there are any *special* instructions, such as a choice of questions to be answered, make sure that you note this instruction carefully.

2) When you are ready to start work on the examination, that is as soon as the signal has been given, read the instructions to each question booklet, underline any key words or phrases, such as *least, best, outline, describe* and the like. In this way you will tend to answer as requested rather than discover on reviewing your paper that you *listed without describing*, that you selected the *worst* choice rather than the *best* choice, etc.

3) If the examination is of the objective or multiple-choice type – that is, each question will also give a series of possible answers: A, B, C or D, and you are called upon to select the best answer and write the letter next to that answer on your answer paper – it is advisable to start answering each question in turn. There may be anywhere from 50 to 100 such questions in the three or four hours allotted and you can see how much time would be taken if you read through all the questions before beginning to answer any. Furthermore, if you come across a question or group of questions which you know would be difficult to answer, it would undoubtedly affect your handling of all the other questions.

4) If the examination is of the essay type and contains but a few questions, it is a moot point as to whether you should read all the questions before starting to answer any one. Of course, if you are given a choice – say five out of seven and the like – then it is essential to read all the questions so you can eliminate the two that are most difficult. If, however, you are asked to answer all the questions, there may be danger in trying to answer the easiest one first because you may find that you will spend too much time on it. The best technique is to answer the first question, then proceed to the second, etc.

5) Time your answers. Before the exam begins, write down the time it started, then add the time allowed for the examination and write down the time it must be completed, then divide the time available somewhat as follows:

- If 3-1/2 hours are allowed, that would be 210 minutes. If you have 80 objective-type questions, that would be an average of 2-1/2 minutes per question. Allow yourself no more than 2 minutes per question, or a total of 160 minutes, which will permit about 50 minutes to review.
- If for the time allotment of 210 minutes there are 7 essay questions to answer, that would average about 30 minutes a question. Give yourself only 25 minutes per question so that you have about 35 minutes to review.

6) The most important instruction is to *read each question* and make sure you know what is wanted. The second most important instruction is to *time yourself properly* so that you answer every question. The third most important instruction is to *answer every question*. Guess if you have to but include something for each question. Remember that you will receive no credit for a blank and will probably receive some credit if you write something in answer to an essay question. If you guess a letter – say "B" for a multiple-choice question – you may have guessed right. If you leave a blank as an answer to a multiple-choice question, the examiners may respect your feelings but it will not add a point to your score. Some exams may penalize you for wrong answers, so in such cases *only*, you may not want to guess unless you have some basis for your answer.

7) Suggestions
   a. Objective-type questions
      1. Examine the question booklet for proper sequence of pages and questions
      2. Read all instructions carefully
      3. Skip any question which seems too difficult; return to it after all other questions have been answered
      4. Apportion your time properly; do not spend too much time on any single question or group of questions
      5. Note and underline key words – *all, most, fewest, least, best, worst, same, opposite*, etc.
      6. Pay particular attention to negatives
      7. Note unusual option, e.g., unduly long, short, complex, different or similar in content to the body of the question
      8. Observe the use of "hedging" words – *probably, may, most likely*, etc.
      9. Make sure that your answer is put next to the same number as the question
      10. Do not second-guess unless you have good reason to believe the second answer is definitely more correct
      11. Cross out original answer if you decide another answer is more accurate; do not erase until you are ready to hand your paper in
      12. Answer all questions; guess unless instructed otherwise
      13. Leave time for review

   b. Essay questions
      1. Read each question carefully
      2. Determine exactly what is wanted. Underline key words or phrases.
      3. Decide on outline or paragraph answer

4. Include many different points and elements unless asked to develop any one or two points or elements
5. Show impartiality by giving pros and cons unless directed to select one side only
6. Make and write down any assumptions you find necessary to answer the questions
7. Watch your English, grammar, punctuation and choice of words
8. Time your answers; don't crowd material

8) Answering the essay question

Most essay questions can be answered by framing the specific response around several key words or ideas. Here are a few such key words or ideas:

M's: manpower, materials, methods, money, management
P's: purpose, program, policy, plan, procedure, practice, problems, pitfalls, personnel, public relations
   a. Six basic steps in handling problems:
     1. Preliminary plan and background development
     2. Collect information, data and facts
     3. Analyze and interpret information, data and facts
     4. Analyze and develop solutions as well as make recommendations
     5. Prepare report and sell recommendations
     6. Install recommendations and follow up effectiveness

   b. Pitfalls to avoid
     1. *Taking things for granted* – A statement of the situation does not necessarily imply that each of the elements is necessarily true; for example, a complaint may be invalid and biased so that all that can be taken for granted is that a complaint has been registered
     2. *Considering only one side of a situation* – Wherever possible, indicate several alternatives and then point out the reasons you selected the best one
     3. *Failing to indicate follow up* – Whenever your answer indicates action on your part, make certain that you will take proper follow-up action to see how successful your recommendations, procedures or actions turn out to be
     4. *Taking too long in answering any single question* – Remember to time your answers properly

IX. AFTER THE TEST

Scoring procedures differ in detail among civil service jurisdictions although the general principles are the same. Whether the papers are hand-scored or graded by machine we have described, they are nearly always graded by number. That is, the person who marks the paper knows only the number – never the name – of the applicant. Not until all the papers have been graded will they be matched with names. If other tests, such as training and experience or oral interview ratings have been given, scores will be combined. Different parts of the examination usually have different weights. For example, the written test might count 60 percent of the final grade, and a rating of training and experience 40 percent. In many jurisdictions, veterans will have a certain number of points added to their grades.

After the final grade has been determined, the names are placed in grade order and an eligible list is established. There are various methods for resolving ties between those who get the same final grade – probably the most common is to place first the name of the person whose application was received first. Job offers are made from the eligible list in the order the names appear on it. You will be notified of your grade and your rank as soon as all these computations have been made. This will be done as rapidly as possible.

People who are found to meet the requirements in the announcement are called "eligibles." Their names are put on a list of eligible candidates. An eligible's chances of getting a job depend on how high he stands on this list and how fast agencies are filling jobs from the list.

When a job is to be filled from a list of eligibles, the agency asks for the names of people on the list of eligibles for that job. When the civil service commission receives this request, it sends to the agency the names of the three people highest on this list. Or, if the job to be filled has specialized requirements, the office sends the agency the names of the top three persons who meet these requirements from the general list.

The appointing officer makes a choice from among the three people whose names were sent to him. If the selected person accepts the appointment, the names of the others are put back on the list to be considered for future openings.

That is the rule in hiring from all kinds of eligible lists, whether they are for typist, carpenter, chemist, or something else. For every vacancy, the appointing officer has his choice of any one of the top three eligibles on the list. This explains why the person whose name is on top of the list sometimes does not get an appointment when some of the persons lower on the list do. If the appointing officer chooses the second or third eligible, the No. 1 eligible does not get a job at once, but stays on the list until he is appointed or the list is terminated.

X. HOW TO PASS THE INTERVIEW TEST

The examination for which you applied requires an oral interview test. You have already taken the written test and you are now being called for the interview test – the final part of the formal examination.

You may think that it is not possible to prepare for an interview test and that there are no procedures to follow during an interview. Our purpose is to point out some things you can do in advance that will help you and some good rules to follow and pitfalls to avoid while you are being interviewed.

What is an interview supposed to test?
The written examination is designed to test the technical knowledge and competence of the candidate; the oral is designed to evaluate intangible qualities, not readily measured otherwise, and to establish a list showing the relative fitness of each candidate – as measured against his competitors – for the position sought. Scoring is not on the basis of "right" and "wrong," but on a sliding scale of values ranging from "not passable" to "outstanding." As a matter of fact, it is possible to achieve a relatively low score without a single "incorrect" answer because of evident weakness in the qualities being measured.

Occasionally, an examination may consist entirely of an oral test – either an individual or a group oral. In such cases, information is sought concerning the technical knowledges and abilities of the candidate, since there has been no written examination for this purpose. More commonly, however, an oral test is used to supplement a written examination.

Who conducts interviews?

The composition of oral boards varies among different jurisdictions. In nearly all, a representative of the personnel department serves as chairman. One of the members of the board may be a representative of the department in which the candidate would work. In some cases, "outside experts" are used, and, frequently, a businessman or some other representative of the general public is asked to serve. Labor and management or other special groups may be represented. The aim is to secure the services of experts in the appropriate field.

However the board is composed, it is a good idea (and not at all improper or unethical) to ascertain in advance of the interview who the members are and what groups they represent. When you are introduced to them, you will have some idea of their backgrounds and interests, and at least you will not stutter and stammer over their names.

What should be done before the interview?

While knowledge about the board members is useful and takes some of the surprise element out of the interview, there is other preparation which is more substantive. It *is* possible to prepare for an oral interview – in several ways:

1) Keep a copy of your application and review it carefully before the interview

This may be the only document before the oral board, and the starting point of the interview. Know what education and experience you have listed there, and the sequence and dates of all of it. Sometimes the board will ask you to review the highlights of your experience for them; you should not have to hem and haw doing it.

2) Study the class specification and the examination announcement

Usually, the oral board has one or both of these to guide them. The qualities, characteristics or knowledges required by the position sought are stated in these documents. They offer valuable clues as to the nature of the oral interview. For example, if the job involves supervisory responsibilities, the announcement will usually indicate that knowledge of modern supervisory methods and the qualifications of the candidate as a supervisor will be tested. If so, you can expect such questions, frequently in the form of a hypothetical situation which you are expected to solve. NEVER go into an oral without knowledge of the duties and responsibilities of the job you seek.

3) Think through each qualification required

Try to visualize the kind of questions you would ask if you were a board member. How well could you answer them? Try especially to appraise your own knowledge and background in each area, *measured against the job sought*, and identify any areas in which you are weak. Be critical and realistic – do not flatter yourself.

4) Do some general reading in areas in which you feel you may be weak

For example, if the job involves supervision and your past experience has NOT, some general reading in supervisory methods and practices, particularly in the field of human relations, might be useful. Do NOT study agency procedures or detailed manuals. The oral board will be testing your understanding and capacity, not your memory.

5) Get a good night's sleep and watch your general health and mental attitude

You will want a clear head at the interview. Take care of a cold or any other minor ailment, and of course, no hangovers.

What should be done on the day of the interview?

Now comes the day of the interview itself. Give yourself plenty of time to get there. Plan to arrive somewhat ahead of the scheduled time, particularly if your appointment is in the fore part of the day. If a previous candidate fails to appear, the board might be ready for you a bit early. By early afternoon an oral board is almost invariably behind schedule if there are many candidates, and you may have to wait. Take along a book or magazine to read, or your application to review, but leave any extraneous material in the waiting room when you go in for your interview. In any event, relax and compose yourself.

The matter of dress is important. The board is forming impressions about you – from your experience, your manners, your attitude, and your appearance. Give your personal appearance careful attention. Dress your best, but not your flashiest. Choose conservative, appropriate clothing, and be sure it is immaculate. This is a business interview, and your appearance should indicate that you regard it as such. Besides, being well groomed and properly dressed will help boost your confidence.

Sooner or later, someone will call your name and escort you into the interview room. *This is it.* From here on you are on your own. It is too late for any more preparation. But remember, you asked for this opportunity to prove your fitness, and you are here because your request was granted.

What happens when you go in?

The usual sequence of events will be as follows: The clerk (who is often the board stenographer) will introduce you to the chairman of the oral board, who will introduce you to the other members of the board. Acknowledge the introductions before you sit down. Do not be surprised if you find a microphone facing you or a stenotypist sitting by. Oral interviews are usually recorded in the event of an appeal or other review.

Usually the chairman of the board will open the interview by reviewing the highlights of your education and work experience from your application – primarily for the benefit of the other members of the board, as well as to get the material into the record. Do not interrupt or comment unless there is an error or significant misinterpretation; if that is the case, do not hesitate. But do not quibble about insignificant matters. Also, he will usually ask you some question about your education, experience or your present job – partly to get you to start talking and to establish the interviewing "rapport." He may start the actual questioning, or turn it over to one of the other members. Frequently, each member undertakes the questioning on a particular area, one in which he is perhaps most competent, so you can expect each member to participate in the examination. Because time is limited, you may also expect some rather abrupt switches in the direction the questioning takes, so do not be upset by it. Normally, a board member will not pursue a single line of questioning unless he discovers a particular strength or weakness.

After each member has participated, the chairman will usually ask whether any member has any further questions, then will ask you if you have anything you wish to add. Unless you are expecting this question, it may floor you. Worse, it may start you off on an extended, extemporaneous speech. The board is not usually seeking more information. The question is principally to offer you a last opportunity to present further qualifications or to indicate that you have nothing to add. So, if you feel that a significant qualification or characteristic has been overlooked, it is proper to point it out in a sentence or so. Do not compliment the board on the thoroughness of their examination – they have been sketchy, and you know it. If you wish, merely say, "No thank you, I have nothing further to add." This is a point where you can "talk yourself out" of a good impression or fail to present an important bit of information. Remember, *you close the interview yourself.*

The chairman will then say, "That is all, Mr. _____, thank you." Do not be startled; the interview is over, and quicker than you think. Thank him, gather your belongings and take your leave. Save your sigh of relief for the other side of the door.

How to put your best foot forward

Throughout this entire process, you may feel that the board individually and collectively is trying to pierce your defenses, seek out your hidden weaknesses and embarrass and confuse you. Actually, this is not true. They are obliged to make an appraisal of your qualifications for the job you are seeking, and they want to see you in your best light. Remember, they must interview all candidates and a non-cooperative candidate may become a failure in spite of their best efforts to bring out his qualifications. Here are 15 suggestions that will help you:

1) Be natural – Keep your attitude confident, not cocky

If you are not confident that you can do the job, do not expect the board to be. Do not apologize for your weaknesses, try to bring out your strong points. The board is interested in a positive, not negative, presentation. Cockiness will antagonize any board member and make him wonder if you are covering up a weakness by a false show of strength.

2) Get comfortable, but don't lounge or sprawl

Sit erectly but not stiffly. A careless posture may lead the board to conclude that you are careless in other things, or at least that you are not impressed by the importance of the occasion. Either conclusion is natural, even if incorrect. Do not fuss with your clothing, a pencil or an ashtray. Your hands may occasionally be useful to emphasize a point; do not let them become a point of distraction.

3) Do not wisecrack or make small talk

This is a serious situation, and your attitude should show that you consider it as such. Further, the time of the board is limited – they do not want to waste it, and neither should you.

4) Do not exaggerate your experience or abilities

In the first place, from information in the application or other interviews and sources, the board may know more about you than you think. Secondly, you probably will not get away with it. An experienced board is rather adept at spotting such a situation, so do not take the chance.

5) If you know a board member, do not make a point of it, yet do not hide it
    Certainly you are not fooling him, and probably not the other members of the board. Do not try to take advantage of your acquaintanceship – it will probably do you little good.

6) Do not dominate the interview
    Let the board do that. They will give you the clues – do not assume that you have to do all the talking. Realize that the board has a number of questions to ask you, and do not try to take up all the interview time by showing off your extensive knowledge of the answer to the first one.

7) Be attentive
    You only have 20 minutes or so, and you should keep your attention at its sharpest throughout. When a member is addressing a problem or question to you, give him your undivided attention. Address your reply principally to him, but do not exclude the other board members.

8) Do not interrupt
    A board member may be stating a problem for you to analyze. He will ask you a question when the time comes. Let him state the problem, and wait for the question.

9) Make sure you understand the question
    Do not try to answer until you are sure what the question is. If it is not clear, restate it in your own words or ask the board member to clarify it for you. However, do not haggle about minor elements.

10) Reply promptly but not hastily
    A common entry on oral board rating sheets is "candidate responded readily," or "candidate hesitated in replies." Respond as promptly and quickly as you can, but do not jump to a hasty, ill-considered answer.

11) Do not be peremptory in your answers
    A brief answer is proper – but do not fire your answer back. That is a losing game from your point of view. The board member can probably ask questions much faster than you can answer them.

12) Do not try to create the answer you think the board member wants
    He is interested in what kind of mind you have and how it works – not in playing games. Furthermore, he can usually spot this practice and will actually grade you down on it.

13) Do not switch sides in your reply merely to agree with a board member
    Frequently, a member will take a contrary position merely to draw you out and to see if you are willing and able to defend your point of view. Do not start a debate, yet do not surrender a good position. If a position is worth taking, it is worth defending.

14) Do not be afraid to admit an error in judgment if you are shown to be wrong

The board knows that you are forced to reply without any opportunity for careful consideration. Your answer may be demonstrably wrong. If so, admit it and get on with the interview.

15) Do not dwell at length on your present job

The opening question may relate to your present assignment. Answer the question but do not go into an extended discussion. You are being examined for a *new* job, not your present one. As a matter of fact, try to phrase ALL your answers in terms of the job for which you are being examined.

Basis of Rating

Probably you will forget most of these "do's" and "don'ts" when you walk into the oral interview room. Even remembering them all will not ensure you a passing grade. Perhaps you did not have the qualifications in the first place. But remembering them will help you to put your best foot forward, without treading on the toes of the board members.

Rumor and popular opinion to the contrary notwithstanding, an oral board wants you to make the best appearance possible. They know you are under pressure – but they also want to see how you respond to it as a guide to what your reaction would be under the pressures of the job you seek. They will be influenced by the degree of poise you display, the personal traits you show and the manner in which you respond.

ABOUT THIS BOOK

This book contains tests divided into Examination Sections. Go through each test, answering every question in the margin. At the end of each test look at the answer key and check your answers. On the ones you got wrong, look at the right answer choice and learn. Do not fill in the answers first. Do not memorize the questions and answers, but understand the answer and principles involved. On your test, the questions will likely be different from the samples. Questions are changed and new ones added. If you understand these past questions you should have success with any changes that arise. Tests may consist of several types of questions. We have additional books on each subject should more study be advisable or necessary for you. Finally, the more you study, the better prepared you will be. This book is intended to be the last thing you study before you walk into the examination room. Prior study of relevant texts is also recommended. NLC publishes some of these in our Fundamental Series. Knowledge and good sense are important factors in passing your exam. Good luck also helps. So now study this Passbook, absorb the material contained within and take that knowledge into the examination. Then do your best to pass that exam.

———

EXAMINATION SECTION

EXAMINATION SECTION
TEST 1

DIRECTIONS: Each question or incomplete statement is followed by several suggested answers or completions. Select the one that BEST answers the question or completes the statement. *PRINT THE LETTER OF THE CORRECT ANSWER IN THE SPACE AT THE RIGHT.*

Questions 1-5

DIRECTIONS: Questions 1 through 5 are to be answered on the basis of the extracts from Federal income tax withholding and social security tax tables shown below. These tables indicate the amounts which must be withheld from the employee's salary by his employer for Federal income tax and for social security. They are based on weekly earnings.

INCOME TAX WITHHOLDING TABLE							
The wages are		And the number of withholding allowances is					
At least	But less than	5	6	7	8	9	10 or more
		The amount of Income tax to be withheld shall be					
$300	$320	$24.60	$19.00	$13.80	$ 8.60	$ 4.00	$ 0
320	340	28.80	22.80	17.40	12.20	7.00	2.80
340	360	33.00	27.00	21.00	15.80	10.60	5.60
360	380	37.20	31.20	25.20	19.40	14.20	9.00
380	400	41.40	35.40	29.40	23.40	17.80	12.60
400	420	45.60	39.60	33.60	27.60	21.40	16.20
420	440	49.80	43.80	37.80	31.80	25.60	19.80
440	460	54.00	48.00	42.00	36.00	29.80	23.80
460	480	58.20	52.20	46.20	40.20	34.00	38.00
480	500	62.40	56.40	50.40	44.40	38.20	32.20

SOCIAL SECURITY TABLE					
WAGES			WAGES		Tax
At least	But less than	Tax to be withheld	At least	But less than	to be withheld
$333.18	$333.52	$19.50	$336.60	$336.94	$19.70
333.52	333.86	19.52	336.94	337.28	19.72
333.86	334.20	19.54	337.28	337.62	19.74
334.20	334.54	19.56	337.62	337.96	19.76
334.54	334.88	19.58	337.96	338.30	19.78
334.88	335.22	19.60	338.30	338.64	19.80
335.22	335.56	19.62	338.64	338.98	19.82
335.56	335.90	19.64	338.98	339.32	19.84
335.90	336.24	19.66	339.32	339.66	19.86
336.24	336.60	19.68	339.66	340.00	19.88

1. If an employee has a weekly wage of $379.50 and claims 6 withholding allowances, the amount of income tax to be withheld is

   A. $27.00   B. $31.20   C. $35.40   D. $37.20

1.__

2. An employee had wages of $335.60 for one week.
With eight withholding allowances claimed, how much income tax will be withheld from his salary?

   A. $8.60   B. $12.20   C. $13.80   D. $17.40

2.__

3. How much social security tax will an employee with weekly wages of $335.60 pay?

   A. $19.60   B. $19.62   C. $19.64   D. $19.66

3.__

4. Mr. Wise earns $339.80 a week and claims seven withholding allowances.
What is his take-home pay after income tax and social security tax are deducted?

   A. $300.32   B. $302.52   C. $319.92   D. $322.40

4.__

5. If an employee pays $19.74 in social security tax and claims eight withholding allowances, the amount of income tax that should be withheld from his wages is

   A. $8.60   B. $12.20   C. $13.80   D. $15.80

5.__

6. A fundamental rule of bookkeeping states that an individual's assets equal his liabilities plus his proprietorship (ASSETS = LIABILITIES + PROPRIETORSHIP).
Which of the following statements logically follows from this rule?

   A. ASSETS = PROPRIETORSHIP - LIABILITIES
   B. LIABILITIES = ASSETS + PROPRIETORSHIP
   C. PROPRIETORSHIP = ASSETS - LIABILITIES
   D. PROPRIETORSHIP = LIABILITIES + ASSETS

6.__

7. Mr. Martin's assets consist of the following:
       Cash on hand: $5,233.74
       Furniture: $4,925.00
       Government Bonds: $5,500.00
What are his TOTAL assets?

   A. $10,158.74   B. $10,425.00
   C. $10,733.74   D. $15,658.74

7.__

8. If Mr. Mitchell has $627.04 in his checking account and then writes three checks for $241.75, $13.24, and $102.97, what will be his new balance?

   A. $257.88   B. $269.08   C. $357.96   D. $369.96

8.__

9. An employee's net pay is equal to his total earnings less all deductions.
If an employee's total earnings in a pay period are $497.05, what is his NET pay if he has the following deductions:
Federal income tax, $90.32; FICA, $28.74; State tax, $18.79; City tax, $7.25; Pension, $1.88?

   A. $351.17   B. $351.07   C. $350.17   D. $350.07

9.__

10. A petty cash fund had an opening balance of $85.75 on December 1. Expenditures of $23.00, $15.65, $5.23, $14.75, and $26.38 were made out of this fund during the first 14 days of the month. Then, on December 17, another $38.50 was added to the fund. If additional expenditures of $17.18, $3.29, and $11.64 were made during the remainder of the month, what was the FINAL balance of the petty cash fund at the end of December?   10.____

   A. $6.93   B. $7.13   C. $46.51   D. $91.40

Questions 11-15.

DIRECTIONS: Questions 11 through 15 are to be answered on the basis of the following instructions.

The chart below is used by the loan division of a city retirement system for the following purposes: (1) to calculate the monthly payment a member must pay on an outstanding loan; (2) to calculate how much a member owes on an outstanding loan after he has made a number of payments.

To calculate the amount a member must pay each month in repaying his loan, look at Column II on the chart. You will notice that each entry in Column II corresponds to a number appearing under the *Months* column; for example, 1.004868 corresponds to 1 month, 0.503654 corresponds to 2 months, etc. To calculate the amount a member must pay each month, use the following procedure: multiply the amount of the loan by the entry in Column II which corresponds to the number of months over which the loan will be paid back. For example, if a loan of $200 is taken out for six months, multiply $200 by 0.169518, the entry in Column II which corresponds to six months.

In order to calculate the balance still owed on an outstanding loan, multiply the monthly payment by the number in Column I which corresponds to the number of monthly payments which remain to be paid on the loan. For example, if a member is supposed to pay $106.00 a month for twelve months, after seven payments, five monthly payments remain. To calculate the balance owed on the loan at this point, multiply the $106.00 monthly payment by 4.927807, the number in Column I that corresponds to five months.

Months	Column I	Column II
1	0.995156	1.004868
2	1.985491	0.503654
3	2.971029	0.336584
4	3.951793	0.253050
5	4.927807	0.202930
6	5.899092	0.169518
7	6.865673	0.145652
8	7.827572	0.127754
9	8.784811	0.113833
10	9.737414	0.102697
11	10.685402	0.093586
12	11.628798	0.085993
13	12.567624	0.079570
14	13.501902	0.074064
15	14.431655	0.069292

11. If Mr. Carson borrows $1,500 for eight months, how much will he have to pay back each month?   11.____

    A. $187.16   B. $191.63   C. $208.72   D. $218.65

12. If a member borrows $2,400 for one year, the amount he will have to pay back each month is   12.____

    A. $118.78   B. $196.18   C. $202.28   D. $206.38

13. Mr. Elliott borrowed $1,700 for a period of fifteen months. Each month he will have to pay back   13.____

    A. $117.80   B. $116.96   C. $107.79   D. $101.79

14. Mr. Aylward is paying back a thirteen-month loan at the rate of $173.13 a month. If he has already made six monthly payments, how much does he owe on the outstanding loan?   14.____

    A. $1,027.39   B. $1,178.75   C. $1,188.65   D. $1,898.85

15. A loan was taken out for 15 months, and the monthly payment was $104.75. After two monthly payments, how much was still owed on this loan?   15.____

    A. $515.79   B. $863.89   C. $1,116.76   D. $1,316.46

16. The ABC Corporation had a gross income of $125,500.00 in 2005. Of this, it paid 60% for overhead.   16.____
If the gross income for 2006 increased by $6,500 and the cost of overhead increased to 61% of gross income, how much more did it pay for overhead in 2006 than in 2005?

    A. $1,320   B. $5,220   C. $7,530   D. $8,052

17. After one year, Mr. Richards paid back a total of $1,695.00 as payment for a $1,500.00 loan. All the money paid over $1,500.00 was simple interest. The interest charge was MOST NEARLY   17.____

    A. 13%   B. 11%   C. 9%   D. 7%

18. A checking account has a balance of $253.36.   18.____
If deposits of $36.95, $210.23, and $7.34 and withdrawals of $117.35, $23.37, and $15.98 are made, what is the NEW balance of the account?

    A. $155.54   B. $351.18   C. $364.58   D. $664.58

19. In 2005, the W Realty Company spent 27% of its income on rent. If it earned $97,254.00 in 2005, the amount it paid for rent was   19.____

    A. $26,258.58   B. $26,348.58
    C. $27,248.58   D. $27,358.58

20. Six percent simple annual interest on $2,436.18 is MOST NEARLY   20.____

    A. $145.08   B. $145.17   C. $146.08   D. $146.17

21. Assume that the XYZ Company has $10,402.72 cash on hand. If it pays $699.83 of this for rent, the amount of cash on hand would be

21.____

    A. $9,792.89   B. $9,702.89
    C. $9,692.89   D. $9,602.89

22. On January 31, Mr. Warren's checking account had a balance of $933.68. If he deposited $36.40 on February 2, $126.00 on February 9, and $90.02 on February 16, and wrote no checks during this period, what was the balance of his account on February 17?

22.____

    A. $680.26   B. $681.26   C. $1,186.10   D. $1,187.00

23. Multiplying a number by .75 is the same as

23.____

    A. *multiplying* it by 2/3   B. *dividing* it by 2/3
    C. *multiplying* it by 3/4   D. *dividing* it by 3/4

24. In City Agency A, 2/3 of the employees are enrolled in a retirement system. City Agency B has the same number of employees as Agency A, and 60% of these are enrolled in a retirement system.
If Agency A has a total of 660 employees, how many MORE employees does it have enrolled in a retirement system than does Agency B?

24.____

    A. 36   B. 44   C. 56   D. 66

25. Net Worth is equal to Assets minus Liabilities.
If, at the end of year, a textile company had assets of $98,695.83 and liabilities of $59,238.29, what was its net worth?

25.____

    A. $38,478.54   B. $38,488.64
    C. $39,457.54   D. $48,557.54

KEY (CORRECT ANSWERS)

1.	B	11.	B
2.	B	12.	D
3.	C	13.	A
4.	B	14.	C
5.	B	15.	D
6.	C	16.	B
7.	D	17.	A
8.	B	18.	B
9.	D	19.	A
10.	B	20.	D

21.	B
22.	C
23.	C
24.	B
25.	C

TEST 2

DIRECTIONS: Each question or incomplete statement is followed by several suggested answers or completions. Select the one that BEST answers the question or completes the statement. *PRINT THE LETTER OF THE CORRECT ANSWER IN THE SPACE AT THE RIGHT.*

Questions 1-10.

DIRECTIONS: Questions 1 through 10 below present the identification numbers, initials, and last names of employees enrolled in a city retirement system. You are to choose the option (A, B, C, or D) that has the IDENTICAL identification number, initials, and last name as those given in each question.

Sample Question
B145698 JL Jones
    A. B146798 JL Jones   B. B145698 JL Jonas
    C. P145698 JL Jones   D. B145698 JL Jones

The correct answer is D. Only Option D shows the identification number, initials, and last name exactly as they are in the sample question. Options A, B, and C have errors in the identification number or last name.

1. J297483 PL Robinson   1.___

    A. J294783 PL Robinson   B. J297483 PL Robinson
    C. J297483 PI Robinson   D. J297843 PL Robinson

2. S497662 JG Schwartz   2.___

    A. S497662 JG Schwarz   B. S497762 JG Schwartz
    C. S497662 JG Schwartz   D. S497663 JG Schwartz

3. G696436 LN Alberton   3.___

    A. G696436 LM Alberton   B. G696436 LN Albertson
    C. G696346 LN Albertson   D. G696436 LN Alberton

4. R774923 AD Aldrich   4.___

    A. R774923 AD Aldrich   B. R744923 AD Aldrich
    C. R774932 AP Aldrich   D. R774932 AD Allrich

5. N239638 RP Hrynyk   5.___

    A. N236938 PR Hrynyk   B. N236938 RP Hrynyk
    C. N239638 PR Hrynyk   D. N239638 RP Hrynyk

6. R156949 LT Carlson   6.___

    A. R156949 LT Carlton   B. R156494 LT Carlson
    C. R159649 LT Carlton   D. R156949 LT Carlson

7. T524697 MN Orenstein   7.___

    A. T524697 MN Orenstein   B. T524967 MN Orinstein
    C. T524697 NM Ornstein   D. T524967 NM Orenstein

8. L346239 JD Remsen   8.____

     A. L346239 JD Remson   B. L364239 JD Remsen
     C. L346329 JD Remsen   D. L346239 JD Remsen

9. P966438 SB Rieperson   9.____

     A. P996438 SB Reiperson   B. P966438 SB Reiperson
     C. R996438 SB Rieperson   D. P966438 SB Rieperson

10. D749382 CD Thompson   10.____

     A. P749382 CD Thompson   B. D749832 CD Thomsonn
     C. D749382 CD Thompson   D. D749823 CD Thomspon

Questions 11-20.

DIRECTIONS: Assume that each of the capital letters in the table below represents the name of an employee enrolled in the city's employees' personnel system. The number directly beneath the letter represents the agency for which the employee works, and the small letter directly beneath represents the code for the employee's account.

Name of Employee	L	O	T	Q	A	M	R	N	C
Agency	3	4	5	9	8	7	2	1	6
Account Code	r	f	b	i	d	t	g	e	n

In each of the following Questions 11 through 20, the agency code numbers and the account code letters in Columns 2 and 3 should correspond to the capital letters in Column 1 and should be in the same consecutive order. For each question, look at each column carefully and mark your answer as follows:

If there are one or more errors in Column 2 *only,* mark your answer A.
If there are one or more errors in Column 3 *only,* mark your answer B.
If there are one or more errors in Column 2 and one or more errors in Column 3, mark your answer C.
If there are NO errors in either column, mark your answer D.

SAMPLE QUESTION

Column 1	Column 2	Column 3
T Q L M O C	5 8 3 7 4 6	b i r t f n

In Column 2, the second agency code number (corresponding to letter Q) should be 9, not 8. Column 3 is coded correctly to Column 1. Since there is an error only in Column 2, the correct answer is A.

	COLUMN 1	COLUMN 2	COLUMN 3	
11.	Q L N R C A	9 3 1 2 6 8	i r e g n d	11.___
12.	N R M O T C	1 2 7 5 4 6	e g f t b n	12.___
13.	R C T A L M	2 6 5 8 3 7	g n d b r t	13.___
14.	T A M L O N	5 7 8 3 4 1	b d t r f e	14.___
15.	A N T O R M	8 1 5 4 2 7	d e b i g t	15.___
16.	M R A L O N	7 2 8 3 4 1	t g d r f e	16.___
17.	C T N Q R O	6 5 7 9 2 4	n d e i g f	17.___
18.	Q M R O T A	9 7 2 4 5 8	i t g f b d	18.___
19.	R Q M C O L	2 9 7 4 6 3	g i t n f r	19.___
20.	N O M R T Q	1 4 7 2 5 9	e f t g b i	20.___

Questions 21-25.

DIRECTIONS: Questions 21 through 25 are to be answered SOLELY on the basis of the following passage.

The city may issue its own bonds or it may purchase bonds as an investment. Bonds may be issued in various denominations, and the face value of the bond is its par value. Before purchasing a bond, the investor desires to know the rate of income that the investment will yield. In computing the yield on a bond, it is assumed that the investor will keep the bond until the date of maturity, except for callable bonds which are not considered in this passage. To compute exact yield is a complicated mathematical problem, and scientifically prepared tables are generally used to avoid such computation. However, the approximate yield can be computed much more easily. In computing approximate yield, the accrued interest on the date of purchase should be ignored because the buyer who pays accrued interest to the seller receives it again at the next interest date. Bonds bought at a premium (which cost more) yield a lower rate of income than the same bonds bought at par (face value), and bonds bought at a discount (which cost less) yield a higher rate of income than the same bonds bought at par.

21. An investor bought a $10,000 city bond paying 6% interest. Which of the following purchase prices would indicate that the bond was bought at a premium?   21.__

   A. $9,000   B. $9,400   C. $10,000   D. $10,600

22. During 2006, a particular $10,000 bond paying 7 1/2% sold at fluctuating prices. Which of the following prices would indicate that the bond was bought at a discount?   22.__

   A. $9,800   B. $10,000   C. $10,200   D. $10,750

23. A certain group of bonds was sold in denominations of $5,000, $10,000, $20,000, and   23.____
    $50,000.
    In the following list of four purchase prices, which one is MOST likely to represent a
    bond sold at par value?

    A. $10,500   B. $20,000   C. $22,000   D. $49,000

24. When computing the approximate yield on a bond, it is DESIRABLE to   24.____

    A. assume the bond was purchased at par
    B. consult scientifically prepared tables
    C. ignore accrued interest on the date of purchase
    D. wait until the bond reaches maturity

25. Which of the following is MOST likely to be an exception to the information provided in   25.____
    the above passage?
    Bonds

    A. purchased at a premium   B. sold at par
    C. sold before maturity   D. which are callable

_____

KEY (CORRECT ANSWERS)

1.	B		11.	D
2.	C		12.	C
3.	D		13.	B
4.	A		14.	A
5.	D		15.	B
6.	D		16.	D
7.	A		17.	C
8.	D		18.	D
9.	D		19.	A
10.	C		20.	D

21.	D
22.	A
23.	B
24.	C
25.	D

_____

TEST 3

DIRECTIONS: Each question or incomplete statement is followed by several suggested answers or completions. Select the one that BEST answers the question or completes the statement. *PRINT THE LETTER OF THE CORRECT ANSWER IN THE SPACE AT THE RIGHT.*

Questions 1-6.

DIRECTIONS: Questions 1 through 6 consist of computations of addition, subtraction, multiplication, and division. For each question, do the computation indicated, and choose the correct answer from the four choices given.

1. ADD: 8936
         7821
         8953
         4297
         9785
         6579

    A. 45371   B. 45381   C. 46371   D. 46381   1.___

2. SUBTRACT: 95,432
             67,596

    A. 27,836   B. 27,846   C. 27,936   D. 27,946   2.___

3. MULTIPLY: 987
              867

    A. 854609   B. 854729   C. 855709   D. 855729   3.___

4. DIVIDE: 59)321439.0

    A. 5438.1   B. 5447.1   C. 5448.1   D. 5457.1   4.___

5. DIVIDE: .057)721

    A. 12,648.0   B. 12,648.1   C. 12,649.0   D. 12,649.1   5.___

6. ADD: 1/2 + 5/7

    A. 1 3/14   B. 1 2/7   C. 1 5/14   D. 1 3/7   6.___

7. If the total number of employees in one city agency increased from 1,927 to 2,006 during a certain year, the percentage increase in the number of employees for that year is MOST NEARLY   7.___

    A. 4%   B. 5%   C. 6%   D. 7%

8. During a single fiscal year, which totaled 248 workdays, one account clerk verified 1,488   8.____
purchase vouchers. Assuming a normal work week of five days, what is the average
number of vouchers verified by the account clerk in a one-week period during this fiscal
year?

   A. 25   B. 30   C. 35   D. 40

9. If the city department of purchase bought 190 computers for $793.50 each and 208 com-   9.____
puters for $839.90 each, the TOTAL price paid for these computers is

   A. $315,813.00   B. $325,464.20
   C. $334,278.20   D. $335.863.00

Questions 10-14.

DIRECTIONS: Questions 10 through 14 are to be answered SOLELY on the basis of the information given in the following paragraph.

Since discounts are in common use in the commercial world and apply to purchases made
by government agencies as well as business firms, it is essential that individuals in both public
and private employment who prepare bills, check invoices, prepare payment vouchers, or write
checks to pay bills have an understanding of the terms used. These include cash or time discount, trade discount, and discount series. A cash or time discount offers a reduction in price to
the buyer for the prompt payment of the bill and is usually expressed as a percentage with a
time requirement, stated in days, within which the bill must be paid in order to earn the discount.
An example would be 3/10, meaning a 3% discount may be applied to the bill if the payment is
forwarded to the vendor within ten days. On an invoice, the cash discount terms are usually followed by the net terms, which is the time in days allowed for ordinary payment of the bill. Thus,
3/10, Net 30 means that full payment is expected in thirty days if the cash discount of 3% is not
taken for having paid the bill within ten days. When the expression Terms Net Cash is listed on
a bill, it means that no deduction for early payment is allowed. A trade discount is normally
applied to list prices by a manufacturer to show the actual price to retailers so that they may
know their cost and determine markups that will allow them to operate competitively and at a
profit. A trade discount is applied by the seller to the list price and is independent of a cash or
time discount. Discounts may also be used by manufacturers to adjust prices charged to retailers without changing list prices. This is usually done by series discounting and is expressed as
a series of percentages. To compute a series discount, such as 40%, 20%, 10%, first apply the
40% discount to the list price, then apply the 20% discount to the remainder, and finally apply
the 10% discount to the second remainder.

10. According to the above passage, trade discounts are   10.____

   A. applied by the buyer
   B. independent of cash discounts
   C. restricted to cash sales
   D. used to secure rapid payment of bills

11. According to the above passage, if the sales terms 5/10, Net 60 appear on a bill in the   11.____
amount of $100 dated December 5, 2006 and the buyer submits his payment on Decem-
ber 15, 2006, his PROPER payment should be

   A. $60   B. $90   C. $95   D. $100

12. According to the above passage, if a manufacturer gives a trade discount of 40% for an item with a list price of $250 and the terms are Net Cash, the price a retail merchant is required to pay for this item is

    A. $250   B. $210   C. $150   D. $100

12.___

13. According to the above passage, a series discount of 25%, 20%, 10% applied to a list price of $200 results in an ACTUAL price to the buyer of

    A. $88   B. $90   C. $108   D. $110

13.___

14. According to the above passage, if a manufacturer gives a trade discount of 50% and the terms are 6/10, Net 30, the cost to a retail merchant of an item with a list price of $500 and for which he takes the time discount is

    A. $220   B. $235   C. $240   D. $250

14.___

Questions 15-22.

DIRECTIONS: Questions 15 through 22 each show in Column I the information written on five cards (lettered j, k, l, m, n) which have to be filed. You are to choose the option (lettered A, B, C, or D) in Column II which BEST represents the proper order of filing according to the information, rules, and sample question given below.

A file card record is kept of the work assignments for all the employees in a certain bureau. On each card is the employee's name, the date of work assignment, and the work assignment code number. The cards are to be filed according to the following rules:

FIRST: File in alphabetical order according to employee's name.

SECOND: When two or more cards have the same employee's name, file according to the assignment date, beginning with the earliest date.

THIRD: When two or more cards have the same employee's name and the same date, file according to the work assignment number beginning with the lowest number.

Column II shows the cards arranged in four different orders. Pick the option (A, B, C, or D) in Column II which shows the correct arrangement of the cards according to the above filing rules.

SAMPLE QUESTION

Column I		Column II	
j.	Cluney 4/8/02 (486503)	A.	k, l, m, j, n
k.	Roster 5/10/01 (246611)	B.	k, n, j, l, m
l.	Altool 10/15/02 (711433)	C.	l, k, j, m, n
m.	Cluney 12/18/02 (527610)	D.	l, n, j, m, k
n.	Cluney 4/8/02 (486500)		

The correct way to file the cards is:

    l.   Altool 10/15/02 (711433)
    n.   Cluney 4/8/02 (486500)
    j.   Cluney 4/8/02 (486503)
    m. Cluney 12/18/02 (527610)
    k.   Roster 5/10/01 (246611)

The correct filing order is shown by the letters l, n, j, m, k. The answer to the sample question is the letter D, which appears in front of the letters l, n, j, m, k in Column II.

	COLUMN I	COLUMN II	
15.	j. Smith 3/19/03 (662118) k. Turner 4/16/99 (481349) l. Terman 3/20/02 (210229) m. Smyth 3/20/02 (481359) n. Terry 5/11/01 (672128)	A. j, m, l, n, k B. j, l, n, m, k C. k, n, m, l, j D. j, n, k, l, m	15.____
16.	j. Ross 5/29/02 (396118) k. Rosner 5/29/02 (439281) l. Rose 7/19/02 (723456) m. Rosen 5/29/03 (829692) n. Ross 5/29/02 (399118)	A. l, m, k, n, j B. m, l, k, n, j C. l, m, k, j, n D. m, l, j, n, k	16.____
17.	j. Sherd 10/12/99 (552368) k. Snyder 11/12/99 (539286) l. Shindler 10/13/98 (426798) m. Scherld 10/12/99 (552386) n. Schneider 11/12/99 (798213)	A. n, m, k, j, l B. j, m, l, k, n C. m, k, n, j, l D. m, n, j, l, k	17.____
18.	j. Carter 1/16/02 (489636) k. Carson 2/16/01 (392671) l. Carter 1/16/01 (486936) m. Carton 3/15/00 (489639) n. Carson 2/16/01 (392617)	A. k, n, j, l, m B. n, k, m, l, j C. n, k, l, j, m D. k, n, l, j, m	18.____
19.	j. Thomas 3/18/99 (763182) k. Tompkins 3/19/00 (928439) l. Thomson 3/21/00 (763812) m. Thompson 3/18/99 (924893) n. Tompson 3/19/99 (928793)	A. m, l, j, k, n B. j, m, l, k, n C. j, l, n, m, k D. l, m, j, n, k	19.____
20.	j. Breit 8/10/03 (345612) k. Briet 5/21/00 (837543) l. Bright 9/18/99 (931827) m. Breit 3/7/98 (553984) n. Brent 6/14/04 (682731)	A. m, j, n, k, l B. n, m, j, k, l C. m, j, k, l, n D. j, m, k, l, n	20.____
21.	j. Roberts 10/19/02 (581932) k. Rogers 8/9/00 (638763) l. Rogerts 7/15/97 (105689) m. Robin 3/8/92 (287915) n. Rogers 4/2/04 (736921)	A. n, k, l, m, j B. n, k, l, j, m C. k, n, l, m, j D. j, m, k, n, l	21.____

	COLUMN I	COLUMN II

22.
- j. Hebert 4/28/02 (719468)
- k. Herbert 5/8/01 (938432)
- l. Helbert 9/23/04 (832912)
- m. Herbst 7/10/03 (648599)
- n. Herbert 5/8/01 (487627)

A. n, k, j, m, l
B. j, l, n, k, m
C. l, j, k, n, m
D. l, j, n, k, m

22.___

23. In order to pay its employees, the Convex Company obtained bills and coins in the following denominations:

Denomination	$20	$10	$5	$1	$.50	$.25	$.10	$.05	$.01
Number	317	122	38	73	69	47	39	25	36

What was the TOTAL amount of cash obtained?

A. $7,874.76
C. $7,889.25
B. $7,878.00
D. $7,924.35

23.___

24. H. Partridge receives a weekly gross salary (before deductions) of $596.25. Through weekly payroll deductions of $19.77, he is paying back a loan he took from his pension fund.
If other fixed weekly deductions amount to $184.14, how much pay would Mr. Partridge take home over a period of 33 weeks?

A. $11,446.92
C. $12,947.22
B. $12,375.69
D. $19,676.25

24.___

25. Mr. Robertson is a city employee enrolled in a city retirement system. He has taken out a loan from the retirement fund and is paying it back at the rate of $14.90 every two weeks. In eighteen weeks, how much money will he have paid back on the loan?

A. $268.20   B. $152.80   C. $134.10   D. $67.05

25.___

26. In 2005, the Iridor Book Company had the following expenses: rent, $6,500; overhead, $52,585; inventory, $35,700; and miscellaneous, $1,275.
If all of these expenses went up 18% in 2006, what would they TOTAL in 2006?

A. $17,290.80
C. $96,060.00
B. $78,769.20
D. $113,350.80

26.___

27. Ms. Ranier had a gross salary of $355.36, paid once every week.
If the deductions from each paycheck are $62.72, $25.13, $6.29, and $1.27, how much money would Ms. Ranier take home in four weeks?

A. $1,039.80
C. $2,079.60
B. $1,421.44
D. $2,842.88

27.___

28. Mr. Martin had a net income of $19,100 for the year. If he spent 34% on rent and household expenses, 3% on house furnishings, 25% on clothes, and 36% on food, how much was left for savings and other expenses?

A. $196.00   B. $382.00   C. $649.40   D. $1960.00

28.___

29. Mr. Elsberg can pay back a loan of $1,800 from the city employees' retirement system if   29.____
    he pays back $36.69 every two weeks for two full years.
    At the end of the two years, how much more than the original $1,800 he borrowed will
    Mr. Elsberg have paid back?

    A. $53.94   B. $107.88   C. $190.79   D. $214.76

30. Mrs. Nusbaum is a city employee, receiving a gross salary (salary before deductions) of   30.____
    $31,200. Every two weeks, the following deductions are taken out of her salary: Federal
    Income Tax, $243.96; FICA, $66.39; State Tax, $44.58; City Tax, $20.91; Health
    Insurance, $4.71.
    If Mrs.Nusbaum's salary and deductions remained the same for a full calendar year,
    what would her NET salary (gross salary less deductions) be in that year?

    A. $9,894.30   B. $21,305.70
    C. $28,118.25   D. $30,819.45

KEY (CORRECT ANSWERS)

1.	C		16.	C
2.	A		17.	D
3.	D		18.	C
4.	C		19.	B
5.	D		20.	A
6.	A		21.	D
7.	A		22.	B
8.	B		23.	A
9.	B		24.	C
10.	B		25.	C
11.	C		26.	D
12.	C		27.	A
13.	C		28.	B
14.	B		29.	B
15.	A		30.	B

ARITHMETIC

EXAMINATION SECTION
TEST 1

DIRECTIONS: Each question or incomplete statement is followed by several suggested answers or completions. Select the one that BEST answers the question or completes the statement. *PRINT THE LETTER OF THE CORRECT ANSWER IN THE SPACE AT THE RIGHT.*

1. 575 x 269 =   1.____

    A. 156,475   B. 154,765
    C. 154,675   D. none of the above

2. 837 x 720 =   2.____

    A. 602,640   B. 602,460
    C. 620,460   D. none of the above

3. 414 x 961 =   3.____

    A. 397,854   B. 397,845
    C. 397,485   D. none of the above

4. 898 x 303 =   4.____

    A. 272,049   B. 272,904
    C. 272,194   D. none of the above

5. 5,623 x 2,183 =   5.____

    A. 12,275,099   B. 12,275,009
    C. 12,276,009   D. none of the above

6. 913.67 x 1.04 =   6.____

    A. 950.1628   B. 9502.168
    C. 950.2168   D. none of the above

7. 313 x 2.78 =   7.____

    A. 870.41   B. 870.14
    C. 870.10   D. none of the above

8.   69   8.____
     23
     12
  +14

    A. 117   B. 118
    C. 120   D. none of the above

9.   318   9.____
   902
    45
  +18

    A. 1,228   B. 1,282
    C. 1,828   D. none of the above

10.　$ 78.50
　　　　.65
　　118.20
　　　7.07

A.　$204.42
C.　$214.42

B.　$214.43
D.　none of the above

11.　8.6809
　　　.7516
　+ 1.5403

A.　10.9787
C.　10.9728

B.　10.9738
D.　none of the above

12.　　53
　　781
　　　60
　+199

A.　1,003
C.　1,093

B.　1,099
D.　none of the above

13.　6 1/8
　　4 2/3
　+9 1/6

A.　19 23/24
C.　19 21/24

B.　20 11/12
D.　none of the above

14.　2 1/2
　　8 1/4
　+7 1/6

A.　17 5/6
C.　18 1/12

B.　17 11/13
D.　none of the above

15.　$ 463.57
　　-84.68

A.　$378.88
C.　$378.89

B.　$388.89
D.　none of the above

16.　$ 1,682.40
　　-834.12

A.　$848.82
C.　$884.28

B.　$848.22
D.　none of the above

17.　991.17
　　-916.68

A.　74.99
C.　79.99

B.　74.49
D.　none of the above

18.
6,241
- 861
─────

    A.   5,480   B.   5,380
    C.   5,408   D.   none of the above

19.
8971.6
- 333.3
──────

    A.   8648.3   B.   8638.3
    C.   8683.3   D.   none of the above

20.
39 1/ 4
- 7 1/ 2
──────

    A.   31 1/2   B.   31 3/4
    C.   30 1/2   D.   none of the above

21. $6\sqrt{5052}$ =

    A.   842   B.   804
    C.   844   D.   none of the above

22. $12\sqrt{7596}$ =

    A.   630   B.   603
    C.   636   D.   none of the above

23. $14\sqrt{368.501}$ =

    A.   26.3251   B.   25.3255
    C.   26.3215   D.   none of the above

24. $21\sqrt{391.73}$ =

    A.   18.654 (approximately)   B.   18.653 (approximately)
    C.   18.635 (approximately)   D.   none of the above

25. $5 \cdot 4\sqrt{175.5}$ =

    A.   325.4   B.   32.45
    C.   33.55   D.   none of the above

26. $2\sqrt{8\ 3/ 8}$ =

    A.   4 7/16   B.   4 3/4
    C.   4 3/16   D.   none of the above

27. $6\sqrt{25\ 4/ 5}$ =

    A.   4 3/10   B.   4 2/5
    C.   4 1/3   D.   none of the above

28. Change the following to decimal form $\frac{15}{14}$ 28.___

    A. .652   B. .655
    C. .625   D. none of the above

29. Take 1/6 of 372   29.___

    A. 57   B. 48
    C. 62   D. none of the above

30. Take 1/11 of 380.6   30.___

    A. 36.4   B. 34.6
    C. 36.6   D. none of the above

31. Find 7 1/2% of $3600   31.___

    A. $280   B. $270
    C. $275   D. none of the above

32. Find 16% of $215   32.___

    A. $34.40   B. $33.44
    C. $34.04   D. none of the above

33. Find 9 3/4% of 14   33.___

    A. 1.365   B. 1.356
    C. 1.565   D. none of the above

34. Find 3 4/5% of 15.5   34.___

    A. .597   B. .589
    C. .579   D. none of the above

35. Find 28% of $6535   35.___

    A. $1789.40   B. $1839.40
    C. $1788.49   D. none of the above

36. If .25 is divided by 40, the result is   36.___

    A. .00625   B. .0625
    C. .625   D. none of the above

37. The number 40 is 80% of   37.___

    A. 45   B. 50
    C. 55   D. none of the above

38. The number 24 is 60% of   38.___

    A. 30   B. 35
    C. 40   D. none of the above

39. If 9/10 of a number is 54, the number is   39._

    A. 63   B. 60
    C. 74   D. none of the above

40. If 4/7 of a number is 64, the number is   40._____

    A. 122   B. 108
    C. 112   D. none of the above

41. If 45 is divided by .15, the result is   41._____

    A. 30   B. 300
    C. 3000   D. none of the above

42. If 29,021.251 is divided by 61.879, the result is   42._____

    A. 4690   B. 469
    C. 405   D. none of the above

43. If 5,252.52 is divided by 62.53, the result is   43._____

    A. 84   B. 790
    C. 79   D. none of the above

44. If 20% of a number is 62, the number is   44._____

    A. 295   B. 305
    C. 335   D. none of the above

45. If 55% of a number is 220, the number is   45._____

    A. 405   B. 400
    C. 380   D. none of the above

46. If the product of 160 multiplied by .06 is subtracted from the product of 17.5 multiplied by   46._____
.7, the result is

    A. 2.65   B. 3.2
    C. 4.1   D. none of the above

47. Add the following lengths: 3 feet, 2 inches; 4 yards, 8 inches; 6 yards, 10 feet, 3 inches; 8   47._____
feet, 2 inches; and give the answer in feet and fractions thereof.

    A. 52 1/4'   B. 52 1/3'
    C. 53 1/4'   D. None of the above

48. What is the net amount of a bill of $354 after a discount of 12% has been allowed?   48._____

    A. $311.25   B. $311.52
    C. $312.52   D. None of the above

49. What is the net amount of a bill of $675.50 after a discount of 9% has been allowed?   49._____
(approximately)

    A. $641.07   B. $614.07
    C. $614.70   D. None of the above

50. At 6 cents each, the cost of 215 plastic forks would be   50._____

    A. $15.06   B. $18.60
    C. $21.86   D. none of the above

51. The sum of the numbers 46,385, 54,672, 6,210, 4,527, 38,925 is

    A. 150,917   B. 150,719
    C. 170,919   D. none of the above

51.____

52. The sum of the numbers 462, 75,832, 6,731, 60,235, 8,427 is

    A. 143,463   B. 151,687
    C. 174,823   D. none of the above

52.____

53. If a log measuring 8 feet, 4 inches is divided into five equal parts, each part is

    A. 1 foot   B. 1 foot, 1 3/4 inches
    C. 1 foot, 4 1/3 inches   D. none of the above

53.____

54. If erasers are sold at the rate of 5 for 18 cents, then 45 erasers will cost

    A. $1.62   B. $1.72
    C. $1.82   D. none of the above

54.____

55. If erasers are sold at the rate of 4 for 6 cents, then 120 erasers will cost

    A. $1.65   B. $1.75
    C. $1.85   D. none of the above

55.____

KEY (CORRECT ANSWERS)

1. C	16. D	31. B	46. A
2. A	17. A	32. A	47. A
3. A	18. B	33. A	48. B
4. D	19. B	34. B	49. C
5. B	20. B	35. D	50. D
6. C	21. A	36. A	51. B
7. B	22. D	37. B	52. B
8. B	23. C	38. C	53. D
9. D	24. A	39. B	54. A
10. A	25. D	40. C	55. D
11. C	26. C	41. B	
12. C	27. A	42. B	
13. A	28. C	43. A	
14. D	29. C	44. D	
15. C	30. B	45. B	

SOLUTIONS TO PROBLEMS

1. (575)(269) = 154,675

2. (837)(720) = 602,640

3. (414)(961) = 397,854

4. (898)(303) = 272,094

5. (5623X2183) = 12,275,009

6. (913.67X1.04) = 950.2168

7. (313)(2.78) = 870.14

8. 69 + 23 + 12 + 14 = 118

9. 318 + 902 + 45 + 18 = 1283

10. $78.50 + .65 + $118.20 + $7.07 = 204.42

11. 8.6809 + .7516 + 1.5403 = 10.9728

12. 53 + 781 + 60 + 199 = 1093

13. 6 1/8 + 4 2/3 + 9 1/6 = 6 3/24 + 4 16/24 + 9 4/24 = 19 23/24

14. 2 1/2 + 8 1/4 + 7 1/6 = 2 6/12 + 8 3/12 + 7 2/12 = 17 11/12

15. $463.57 - $84.68 = $378.89

16. $1682.40 - $834.12 = $848.28

17. 991.17 - 916.18 = 74.99

18. 6241 - 861 = 5380

19. 8971.6 - 333.3 = 8638.3

20. 39 1/4 - 7 1/2 = 39 1/4 - 7 2/4 = 31 3/4

21. 5052 ÷ 6 = 842

22. 7596 ÷ 12 = 633

23. 368.501 ÷ 14 = 26.3215

24. $391 \cdot 73 \div 21 \approx 18 \cdot 654$

25. $175.5 \div 5.4 = 32.5$

26. $8\frac{3}{4} \div 2 = (\frac{67}{8})(\frac{1}{2}) = \frac{67}{16} = 4\frac{3}{16}$

27. $25\frac{4}{5} \div 6 = (\frac{129}{5})(\frac{1}{6}) = \frac{129}{30} = 4\frac{3}{10}$

28. $15/24 = .625$

29. $(1/6)(372) = 62$

30. $(1/11)(380.6) = 34.6$

31. $(.075)(\$3600) = \$270$

32. $(.16)(\$215) = \$34.40$

33. $9\frac{3}{4}\%$ of $14 = (\cdot 0975)(14) = 1 \cdot 365$

34. $3\ 4/5\%$ of $15.5 = (.038)(15.5) = .589$

35. $(.28)(\$6535) = \$1829.80$

36. $.25 \div 40 = .00625$

37. $40 = 80\%$ of x · Then, $x = 40 \div \cdot 80 = 50$

38. $24 = 60\%$ of x. Then, $x = 24 \div .60 = 40$

39. $9/10$ of $x = 54$. Then, $x = 54 \div 9/10 = 60$

40. $4/7$ of $x = 64$ Then, $x = 64 \div 4/7 = 112$

41. $45 \div .15 = 300$

42. $29{,}021.251 \div 61.879 = 469$

43. $5252.52 \div 62.53 = 84$

44. 20% of $x = 62$. Then, $x = 62 \div .20 = 310$

45. 55% of $x = 220$. Then, $x = 220 \div .55 = 400$

46. (17.5) (.7) - (160)(.06) = 12.25 - 9.6 = 2.65

47. 3 ft. 2 in. + 4 yds. 8 in. + 6 yds. 10 ft. 3 in. + 8 ft. 2 in. = 3 ft. 2 in. + 12 ft. 8 in. + 28 ft. 3 in. + 8 ft. 2 in. = 51 ft. 15 in. = 52 ft. 3 in. = 52 1/4 ft.

48. $354 - (.12)($354) = $354 - $42.48 = $311.52

49. $675.50 - (.09)($675.50) ≈ $675.50 - $60.80 = $614.70

50. (215)(.06) = $12.90

51. 46,385 + 54,672 + 6210 + 4527 + 38,925 = 150,719

52. 462 + 75,832 + 6731 + 60,235 + 8427 = 151,687

53. 8 ft. 4 in. ÷ 5 = 100 in, ÷ 5 = 20 in. = 1 ft. 8 in.

54. Let x = cost. Then, 5/.18 = 45/x , 5x = 8.10, x = $1.62

55. Let x = cost. Then, 4/.06 = 120/x , 4x = 7.20, x = $1.80

ARITHMETIC
EXAMINATION SECTION
TEST 1

DIRECTIONS: Each question or incomplete statement is followed by several suggested answers or completions. Select the one that BEST answers the question or completes the statement. *PRINT THE LETTER OF THE CORRECT ANSWER IN THE SPACE AT THE RIGHT.*

1. $34\overline{)17136}$

   A. 54   B. 503 24/34   C. 504   D. 505 4/34   E. NG

1.____

2. 141606
   -94679

   A. 46,837   B. 46,927   C. 46,937   D. 47,027   E. NG

2.____

3. $86\overline{)8342}$

   A. 96   B. 96 76/86   C. 97 6/86   D. 97 16/86   E. NG

3.____

4. $1\frac{2}{3}$
   $+1\frac{5}{6}$

   A. 2 1/6   B. 2 1/2   C. 3 1/2   D. 3 1/3   E. NG

4.____

5. $3\overline{)128.94}$

   A. 42.98   B. 4.298   C. 429.8   D. 4298   E. NG

5.____

6. 709
   x864

   A. 612,576   B. 602,576   C. 611,576   D. 612,566   E. NG

6.____

7. 138057
   -54368

   A. 83,679   B. 83,689   C. 83,789   D. 84,689   E. NG

7.____

8. $3\frac{3}{5} \div \frac{9}{10} =$

   A. 1/4   B. 2 1/2   C. 2 3/5   D. 3 3/5   E. NG

8.____

9. $7\overline{)21.441}$

   A. 3.063   B. 3.63   C. .363   D. 3063   E. NG

9.____

10. $\frac{9}{10} - \frac{1}{2} =$ 10.____

     A. 3/5   B. 2/5   C. 1/2   D. 1 2/5   E. NG

11. $\frac{2}{3} \times 2\frac{1}{4} =$ 11.____

     A. 1   B. 2 1/2   C. 2   D. 1 1/2   E. NG

12.   7646
      6799
      3389
   +6597   12.____

     A. 23,431   B. 24,331   C. 24,431   D. 24,421   E. NG

13. $\frac{5}{6}$
   $+1\frac{3}{4}$ 13.____

     A. 2 7/12   B. 1 4/5   C. 1 1/12   D. 2 1/2   E. NG

14. Round to tenths: 22.3 - 1.21 =   14.____

     A. 21.0   B. 21.5   C. 21.8   D. 21.9   E. NG

15. Round to 2 digits: 15.____

     9.05
   x 5.9

     A. 53   B. 5.4   C. 5.3   D. 54   E. NG

16.   608
   x970   16.____

     A. 58,776   B. 58,876   C. 588,760   D. 589,760   E. NG

17.   6567
      8999
      6877
   +8789   17.____

     A. 30,232   B. 31,132   C. 31,222   D. 31,232   E. NG

18.   4987
   x 96   18.____

     A. 468,752   B. 477,752   C. 478,742   D. 478,752   E. NG

19.
$$3\frac{1}{3}$$
$$-1\frac{3}{4}$$

19.____

    A. 1 5/12   B. 1 7/12   C. 2 1/2   D. 2 7/12| E. NG

20. What is 4% of $500?

20.____

    A. $20.00   B. $1.25   C. $2.00   D. $80.00   E. NG

21.
$$16$$
$$\times 10\frac{3}{4}$$

21.____

    A. 160   B. 160 3/4   C. 167 1/2   D. 172   E. NG

22. If $\frac{16}{K}=8$, then K =

22.____

    A. 1/2   B. 8   C. 128   D. 2   E. NG

23. Round to tenths:
    4.35
    x0.32

23.____

    A. 1.3   B. 13.9   C. 1.4   D. 14.0   E. NG

24. What is $2\frac{1}{2}$% of $50?

24.____

    A. $12.50   B. $1.25   C. $25.00   D. $125.00   E. NG

25. 89)‾6267.38

25.____

    A. 7.42   B. 74.2   C. 7042   D. 70.42   E. NG

26. $10 is what percent of $400?

26.____

    A. 4   B. 25   C. 2 1/2   D. 40   E. NG

27. .68)‾31.96

27.____

    A. 0.47   B. 47   C. 4.7   D. 470   E. NG

28. $\frac{4}{6}=\frac{N}{24}$

28.____

    A. 6   B. 18   C. 16   D. 36   E. NG

29. 6÷10=

29.____

    A. 2/3   B. 3/5   C. 1 2/3   D. 6   E. NG

30. $\dfrac{3}{10} = \dfrac{15}{N}$

    A. 5   B. 40   C. 45   D. 150   E. NG

30.____

31. $\dfrac{3a}{4} = 6$

    $a =$

    A. 2   B. 24   C. 8   D. 72   E. NG

31.____

32. $40 is what percent of $1600?

    A. 20   B. 6.40   C. 2 1/2   D. 40   E. NG

32.____

33. $25 is 5% of what amount?

    A. $1.25   B. $125.00   C. $5000.00   D. $500.00   E. NG

33.____

34. $\begin{array}{r} (-3) \\ \times\ 6 \\ \hline \end{array}$

    A. 9   B. 15   C. 18   D. -18   E. NG

34.____

35. $160 is 4% of what amount?

    A. $4000.00   B. $64.00   C. $400.00   D. $6.40   E. NG

35.____

36. $\dfrac{N}{12} = \dfrac{13}{39}$

    $N =$

    A. 4   B. 3   C. 13   D. 36   E. NG

36.____

37. $- 4 + 2 =$

    A. -6   B. -2   C. 2   D. 8   E. NG

37.____

38. $5N = 8N - 12$

    $N =$

    A. 5/8   B. 4   C. 3   D. 13   E. NG

38.____

39. $\dfrac{16}{-8} =$

    A. 2   B. 8   C. 12   D. -2   E. NG

39.____

40. $2a - 4 = 14 - a$

    $a =$

    A. 6   B. 3 1/3   C. 5   D. 10   E. NG

40.____

KEY (CORRECT ANSWERS)

1.	C	11.	D	21.	D	31.	C
2.	B	12.	C	22.	D	32.	C
3.	E	13.	A	23.	C	33.	D
4.	C	14.	E	24.	B	34.	D
5.	A	15.	A	25.	D	35.	A
6.	A	16.	D	26.	C	36.	A
7.	B	17.	D	27.	B	37.	B
8.	E	18.	D	28.	C	38.	B
9.	A	19.	B	29.	B	39.	D
10.	B	20.	A	30.	E	40.	A

SOLUTIONS TO PROBLEMS

1. $17,136 \div 34 = 504$

2. $141,606 - 94,679 = 46,927$

3. $8342 \div 86 = 97$

4. $1\frac{2}{3} + 1\frac{5}{6} = 1\frac{4}{6} + 1\frac{5}{6} = 2\frac{9}{6} = 3\frac{1}{2}$

5. $128.94 \div 3 = 42.98$

6. $709 \times 864 = 612,576$

7. $138,057 - 54,368 = 83,689$

8. $3\frac{3}{5} \div \frac{9}{10} = \frac{18}{5} \times \frac{10}{9} = \frac{180}{45} = 4$

9. $21.441 \div 7 = 3.063$

10. $\frac{9}{10} - \frac{1}{2} = \frac{9}{10} - \frac{5}{10} = \frac{4}{10} = \frac{2}{5}$

11. $\frac{2}{3} \times 2\frac{1}{4} = \frac{2}{3} \times \frac{9}{4} = \frac{18}{12} = 1\frac{1}{2}$

12. $7646 + 6799 + 3389 + 6597 = 24,431$

13. $\frac{5}{6} + 1\frac{3}{4} = \frac{10}{12} + 1\frac{9}{12} = 1\frac{19}{12} = 2\frac{7}{12}$

14. $22.3 - 1.21 = 21.09 = 21.1$ rounded to nearest tenth

15. $9.05 \times 5.9 = 53.395 = 53$ rounded to two digits

16. $608 \times 970 = 589,760$

17. $6567 + 8999 + 6877 + 8789 = 31,232$

18. $4987 \times 96 = 478,752$

19. $3\frac{1}{3} - 1\frac{3}{4} = 3\frac{4}{12} - 1\frac{9}{12} = 2\frac{16}{12} - 1\frac{9}{12} = 1\frac{7}{12}$

20. 4% of \$500 = (.04)(\$500) = \$20

21. $16 \times 10\frac{3}{4} = \frac{16}{1} \times \frac{43}{4} = \frac{688}{4} = 172$

22. $\frac{16}{K} = 8$, $16 = 8K$, $K = 2$

23. $4.35 \times .32 = 1.3920 = 1.4$ rounded to nearest tenth

24. $2\frac{1}{2}\%$ of $\$50 = (.025)(\$50) = \$1.25$

25. $6267.38 \div 89 = 70.42$

26. $\frac{\$10}{\$400} = \frac{1}{40} = 2\frac{1}{2}\%$

27. $31.96 \div .68 = 47$

28. $\frac{4}{6} = \frac{N}{24}$, $6N = 96$, $N = 16$

29. $6 \div 10 = \frac{6}{10} = \frac{3}{5}$

30. $\frac{3}{10} = \frac{15}{N}$, $3N = 150$, $N = 50$

31. $\frac{3a}{4} = 6$, $3a = 24$, $a = 8$

32. $\frac{\$40}{\$1600} = \frac{1}{40} = 2\frac{1}{2}\%$

33. $\$25 = 5\%$ of x, $\$25 = .05x$, $x = \frac{\$25}{.05} = \$500$

34. $(-3) \times (6) = -18$

35. $\$160 = 4\%$ of x , $\$160 = .04$, $x = \frac{\$160}{.04} = \$4000$

36. $\frac{N}{12} = \frac{13}{39} = \frac{1}{3}$, $3N = 12$, $N = 4$

37. $-4 + 2 = -2$

38. 5N = 8N - 12, -3N = -12, N = 4

39. $\dfrac{16}{-8}$ = -2

40. 2a - 4 = 14 - a, 3a - 4 = 14, 3a = 18, a = 6

———

TEST 2

DIRECTIONS: Each question or incomplete statement is followed by several suggested answers or completions. Select the one that BEST answers the question or completes the statement. *PRINT THE LETTER OF THE CORRECT ANSWER IN THE SPACE AT THE RIGHT.*

1. 6 is what part of 9?   1._____

    A. 1/6   B. 1/3   C. 2/3   D. 1 1/2

2. What is 1.48 rounded to tenths?   2._____

    A. 1.4   B. 1.5   C. 1.40   D. 1.50

3. If N times 6 is less than 63, then N may be   3._____

    A. 378   B. 69   C. 9   D. 12

4. What is the smallest common denominator for 1/5, 1/2, and 1/3?   4._____

    A. 2   B. 3   C. 30   D. 10

5. What does CXC mean?   5._____

    A. 210   B. 190   C. 200   D. 201

6. $\boxed{} \times 3 = 18.$ 6._____
    Which numbers, if put into the box, would make the sentence TRUE?

    A. 3 x 3   B. 4 + 5   C. 9 - 2   D. 12 + 2

7. Two-thirds of what number is 8?   7._____

    A. 12   B. 2 2/3   C. 16   D. 24

8. What is 2.0094 rounded to the nearest hundredth?   8._____

    A. 2.009   B. 2.01   C. 2.10   D. 2.010

9. Here are decimal fractions written in four bases.   9._____
    Which would be the LARGEST part of the same pie?

    A. 0.3_{four} B. 0.3_{five} C. 0.3_{six} D. 0.3_{eight}

10. Ten thousand is how many hundreds?   10._____

    A. 1   B. 10   C. 1000   D. 100

11. Interest is found by using the formula   11._____

    A. lwh   B. prh   C. prt   D. hrw

12. What number is 200% of 25?   12._____

    A. 4   B. 40
    C. No such number   D. 50

13. What is the value of N in $\dfrac{25}{75} = \dfrac{N}{24}$?   13.____

    A. 3   B. 49   C. 12   D. 8

14. What is the product of 3 x (-4)?   14.____

    A. +12   B. 1/12
    C. -12   D. Can't be multiplied

15. What is the square of (4+2)?   15.____

    A. 36   B. 16   C. 8   D. 6

16. 0.26 x 558 is approximately   16.____

    A. 140   B. 2300   C. 1400   D. 230

17. $\sqrt{1600}$ is equal to   17.____

    A. 4   B. 40   C. 400   D. 4000

18. How many hours pass from 9:45 A.M. to 1:30 P.M.?   18.____

    A. $8\dfrac{1}{4}$ B. $4\dfrac{1}{4}$ C. $4\dfrac{3}{4}$ D. $3\dfrac{3}{4}$

19. Without multiplying, find the difference between 29 x 347 and 28 x 347.   19.____

    A. 1   B. 347   C. 29   D. 28

20. What is the dividend if the quotient is 8 and the divisor is 2?   20.____

    A. 2   B. 4   C. 16   D. 6

21. 5^3 equals   21.____

    A. 15   B. 25   C. 625   D. 125

22. Which fraction is expressed in lowest terms?   22.____

    A. $\dfrac{49}{280}$ B. $\dfrac{99}{301}$ C. $\dfrac{475}{1320}$ D. $\dfrac{998}{1106}$

23. 4 x 253 equals   23.____

    A. (4x3) + (4x5) + (4x2)   B. (4x200) + (4x5) + (4x3)
    C. (4x20) + (4x50) + (4x3)   D. (4x250) + (4x3)

24. Which number comes next in this set: 1248?   24.____

    A. 16   B. 12   C. 14   D. 10

25. Which of these is the BEST estimate of 0.80÷0.04?   25.____

    A. 0.02   B. 0.20   C. 2.0   D. 20

26. By the distributive property of numbers, we know that 246 x z equals   26._____

    A. 2Z + 4Z + 6Z   B. 200Z x 40Z x 6Z
    C. 200Z + 40Z + 6Z   D. 6Z + 4Z + ZZ

27. If (N+4) times 3 is more than 24, you can be sure that N is   27._____

    A. more than 8   B. less than 3
    C. less than 8   D. more than 4

28. There are 2 black balls and 3 white balls in a hat. What are the chances that the first one   28._____
    drawn out will be white?

    A. 1 in 2   B. 3 in 5   C. 2 in 3   D. 1 in 3

29. If N stands for the same number in each of the following, which will be the smallest?   29._____

    A. $N+\dfrac{1}{2}$ B. $N+\dfrac{1}{3}$ C. $N+\dfrac{2}{3}$ D. $N+\dfrac{1}{4}$

30. By the commutative property of numbers, we know that   30._____

    A. $\square + \triangle = \triangle + \square$ B. $\square \times \triangle = \triangle \div \square$

    C. $\square \times \triangle = \triangle + \square$ D. $\square - \triangle = \triangle - \square$

31. By estimation, choose the example which will have the largest quotient.   31._____

    A. $23\overline{)401}$ B. $46\overline{)800}$ C. $23\overline{)400}$ D. $46\overline{)801}$

32. $16\dfrac{2}{3}\%$ of $25 is nearest   32._____

    A. 25¢   B. $4.00   C. $2.50   D. 40¢

33. The volume of a right rectangular prism is found by using the formula   33._____

    A. lw   B. hr^2 C. s^2h D. lwh

34. Which of these is a prime number?   34._____

    A. 109   B. 378   C. 126   D. 417

35. If you know that R + S is less than N, then you know that   35._____

    A. R + 1/2 is greater than N
    B. R + S is greater than 1/2N
    C. 1/2R + 1/2S is less than 1/2N
    D. (1/2R) + S is less than 1/2N

36. Which would tell you that a number is evenly divisible by 9?   36._____

    A. The last two digits.   B. The last three digits
    C. The sum of the digits   D. The number is odd

Questions 37-38.

DIRECTIONS: Questions 37 and 38 are to be answered on the basis of the following sets.

   Set K: Los Angeles, Yosemite, Mr. Whitney
   Set L: Chicago, Denver, Los Angeles, Pittsburgh
   Set M: Mt. McKinley, Pikes Peak, Denver

37.   How many elements (different places) are in the union of the three sets, K, L, and M?   37.____
   A.   3   B.   8   C.   4   D.   11

38.   Which two sets, if any, are disjoint, that is, have no common members?   38.____
   A.   M and L   B.   M and K
   C.   L and K   D.   No two sets

39.   How many x's are there if counted in a base of eight instead of a base of ten?   39.____
   X X X X X X X X X X X X X X X X X X X X X
   A. 25_{eight} B. 21_{eight} C. 26_{eight} D. 168_{eight}

40.   The sum of the digits of a five-place numeral is 24.   40.____
   You know the number is evenly divisible (no remainder) by
   A.   4   B.   3   C.   6   D.   8

KEY (CORRECT ANSWERS)

1.	C	11.	C	21.	D	31.	A
2.	B	12.	D	22.	B	32.	B
3.	C	13.	D	23.	D	33.	D
4.	C	14.	C	24.	A	34.	A
5.	B	15.	A	25.	D	35.	C
6.	D	16.	A	26.	C	36.	C
7.	A	17.	B	27.	D	37.	B
8.	B	18.	D	28.	B	38.	B
9.	A	19.	B	29.	C	39.	A
10.	D	20.	C	30.	A	40.	B

SOLUTIONS TO PROBLEMS

1. $\dfrac{6}{9} = \dfrac{2}{3}$

2. 1.48 = 1.5 rounded to nearest tenth

3. 6N < 63, so N < 10.5; so N may be 9

4. The smallest common denominator for 5, 2, and 3 is 30.

5. CXC = 190

6. $12 \div 2 \times 3 = 18$

7. $\dfrac{2}{3}N = 8$, $N = \dfrac{8}{1} \times \dfrac{3}{2} = 12$

8. 2.0094 = 2.01 rounded to nearest hundredth

9. $.3_{four} = 3 \times 4^{-1} = .75_{ten}$; $.3_{five} = 3 \times 5^{-1} = .6_{ten}$;
   $.3_{six} = 3 \times 6^{-1} = .5_{ten}$; $.3_{eight} = 3 \times 8^{-1} = .375_{ten}$
   Thus, $.3_{four}$ is largest.

10. $10{,}000 \div 100 = 100$

11. I = prt

12. 200% of 25 = (2)(25) = 50

13. $\dfrac{25}{75} = \dfrac{1}{3} = \dfrac{N}{24}$, 3N = 24, N = 8

14. $3 \times (-4) = -12$

15. $(4+2)^2 = 6^2 = 36$

16. $.26 \times 558 = 145.08 \approx 140$

17. $\sqrt{1600} = 40$

18. 9:45 A.M. to 1:30 P.M. $= 3\dfrac{3}{4}$ hours

19. $29 \times 347 - 28 \times 347 = 1 \times 347 = 347$

20. $N \div 2 = 8$, so N = 16

21. $5^3 = 5 \times 5 \times 5 = 125$

22. $\dfrac{99}{301}$ is expressed in lowest terms

23. 4 x 253 = (4x250) + (4x3)

24. 1, 2, 4, 8,.... Each number is double its predecessor. Thus, the fifth number = 16

25. $.80 \div .04 = 20$

26. 246 x Z = 200Z + 40Z + 6Z, using the distributive property.

27. (N+4) x 3 > 24, N + 4 > 8, N > 4

28. Probability of drawing a white ball $= \dfrac{3}{2+3} =$ 3 in 5

29. $N \div \dfrac{2}{3}$ is smallest, provided N > 0

30. $\square \Vdash \triangle = \triangle + \square$, by the commutative property

31. $401 \div 23$ is the largest of the given selections.

32. $16\dfrac{2}{3}\%$ of $\$25 = \dfrac{1}{6} \times \$25 \approx \$4$

33. Volume = lwh

34. 109 is a prime number, since its only divisors are 1 and 109

35. If R + S < N, then 1/2 R + 1/2 S < 1/2 N

36. A number is divisible by 9 if the sum of its digits is divisible by 9.

37. The union of sets K, L, M = {Los Angeles, Yosemite, Mt. Whitney, Chicago, Denver, Pittsburgh, Mt. McKinley, Pikes Peak}, which is 8 elements.

38. Sets M and K are disjoint, that is, they have no common elements.

39. $21_{ten} = 25_{eight}$

40. If the sum of the digits is 24, the number must be divisible by 3, since 24 is divisible by 3.

TEST 3

DIRECTIONS: Each question or incomplete statement is followed by several suggested answers or completions. Select the one that BEST answers the question or completes the statement. *PRINT THE LETTER OF THE CORRECT ANSWER IN THE SPACE AT THE RIGHT.*

1.   What is the volume in cubic inches of the item shown at the right?
   A.   24
   B.   26
   C.   48
   D.   64
   E.   NG

1.____

2.   How much cheaper are a dozen pencils at 49¢ a dozen than a dozen sold at 2 for 9¢?

2.____

   A. $4\frac{1}{2}$ ¢   B.   5¢   C.   54¢   D.   58¢   E.   NG

Questions 3-5.

DIRECTIONS: Questions 3 through 5 are to be answered on the basis of the following chart.

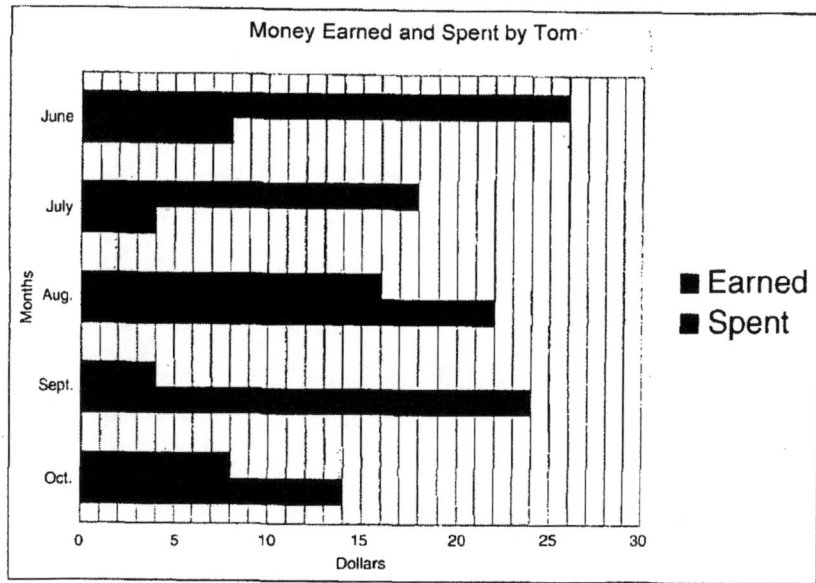

3.   In which month(s) did Tom spend over twice as much as he earned?

3.____

   A.   June and July   B.   August   C.   September
   D.   October   E.   None

4.   How did Tom's earnings compare with what he spent during the 5 months shown?

4.____

   A. $1 more   B.   He broke even
   C. $2 less   D. $3 more
   E.   NG

5. In which month did Tom save the MOST money?   5._____

    A. June   B. July   C. August
    D. September   E. October

Questions 6-11.

DIRECTIONS: Several Scouts went by bus to a national park.Questions 6 through 11 are
              some of their problems.

6. If the bus averages 40 miles per hour for 8 hours, how far will it go in that time?   6._____
    _____ miles.

    A. 5   B. 32   C. 48   D. 320   E. NG

7. At the camp store some candy bars are 3 for 25¢. What would 24 cost at that rate?   7._____

    A. $3.00   B. $4.00   C. $6.00   D. $8.00   E. NG

8. We are scheduled to be home at 6:15 P.M.   8._____
    If the trip home takes 7 1/2 hours, when should we start?
    _____ A.M.

    A. 1:45   B. 8:30   C. 9:45   D. 10:45   E. NG

9. At the park, Bill counted 60 trailers. He estimated that this was 1/3 of the total. 9._____
    If so, what was the TOTAL number of trailers?

    A. 180   B. 30   C. 60   D. 20   E. NG

10. Jerry is drawing a map of the park to send home. A 6-inch line will equal 40 miles of the   10._____
    park.
    His scale will be

    A. 1 in.= 10 mi.   B. $1\frac{1}{2}$ in = $6\frac{2}{3}$ mi.

    C. $1\frac{1}{2}$ in = 10 mi.   D. 2 in.=15 mi.
    E. NG

11. How will the Scouts determine equal shares of the cost?   11._____

    A. Total cost x number of people
    B. Total cost + the average
    C. Number of people x average
    D. Total cost + number of shares

Questions 12-13.

DIRECTIONS: Questions 12 and 13 are to be answered on the basis of the following graph.

DAVID'S DAY (TOTAL 24 HOURS)

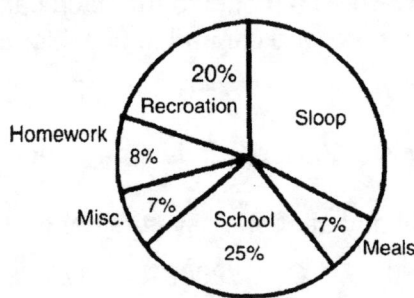

12. What percent of David's day is spent in sleep?   12.____

    A. 33   B. 23   C. 8   D. 37   E. NG

13. How many hours does David spend a day in school?   13.____

    A. 6   B. 7   C. 8   D. 25   E. NG

Questions 14-16.

DIRECTIONS: Questions 14 through 16 are to be answered on the basis of the following chart.

BOXES OF COOKIES SOLD

BOXES OF COOKIES SOLD

Ruth	🍪 🍪 🍪 🍪
Betty	🍪 🍪
Nancy	🍪 🍪 🍪 🍪 🍪 🍪
Sue	🍪 🍪 🍪 🍪 🍪
Mary	🍪 🍪 🍪

Each 🍪 equals 5 boxes

14. Who sold 3 times as many boxes as Betty sold?   14.____

    A. Nancy   B. Ruth   C. Mary   D. Sue   E. No one

15. Sue sold how many more boxes than Ruth sold?   15.____

    A. 1   B. 2   C. 6   D. 15   E. NG

16. How many boxes did Betty sell?   16.____

    A. 2   B. 20   C. 11   D. 10   E. NG

Questions 17-19.

DIRECTIONS: Marvin's mother and father both work downtown. Questions 17 through 19 are some of their problems.

17.   Marvin's mother and father have one car but are considering buying another for $2,000.   17.____
Father figures that it will cost $50.00 a month to run each car.
How much will it cost to buy the second car and to use it for a year?

   A. $2050   B. $2600   C. $2500   D. $3200   E.   NG

18.   The total cost for a babysitter is $7.00 a day for a 5-day week. Mother's take-home pay is   18.____
$3740 for 48 weeks' work.
How much is left of her yearly pay after she pays the babysitter for 48 weeks?

   A. $1480   B. $1680   C. $2060   D. $2140   E.   NG

19.   Father and Mother together earn $12,000 a year. To find how much Father earns a   19.____
month, you would

   A.   divide sum of both salaries by 2; then divide by 12
   B.   subtract Mother's salary from sum of both salaries; multiply by 12
   C.   divide 12 by sum of both salaries; then subtract Mother's salary
   D.   subtract Mother's salary from sum of both; then divide by 12
   E.   do none of the above

20.   What is the circumference of the circle shown in the figure at the right?   20.____

Use $\pi=3\frac{1}{7}$

   A.   11 in.
   B.   21 in.
   C.   22 in.
   D.   154 in.
   E.   NG

Questions 21-23.

DIRECTIONS: Questions 21 through 23 are to be answered on the basis of the following chart.

Number of Problems Worked
and Time Spent

Pupil	Time	Problems
Larry	1'15"	25
Meg	45"	15
Joe	40"	10
Sue	1'30"	30
Bill	50"	25

21. What was the average number of problems worked?   21.____
    A. 15   B. 21   C. 19   D. 25   E. NG

22. What was the median length of time spent?   22.____
    A. 40"   B. 50"   C. 60"   D. 15"   E. NG

23. Who is the fastest worker per problem?   23.____
    A. Meg   B. Sue   C. Joe   D. Bill   E. NG

Questions 24-26.

DIRECTIONS: Jack is planting a hedge 30 feet long. Questions 24 through 26 are some of his
              problems.

24. He can put 30 small plants, costing 15¢ each, 12 inches apart. Or, he can put large   24.____
    plants, costing 40¢ each, 18 inches apart.
    How much more will it cost to buy the large plants?

    A. No more   B. $3.50   C. $4.50   D. $8.00   E. NG

25. Hedge clippers cost $30.00. They can be rented for $1.50 a day. Jack would need them   25.____
    for 4 days each year.
    How many years will it take for the rent to equal the cost?

    A. 4 1/2   B. 5   C. 6   D. 7 1/2   E. NG

26. Jack waters the hedge every day for 15 days, every other day for the next 30 years, and   26.____
    twice a week for the following 16 weeks. Each watering costs about 5¢.
    How much does it cost to water it during this time?

    A. $3.10   B. $3.05   C. $1.90   D. $4.50   E. NG

27. How long is the diagonal line shown in the figure at the right?   27.____
    A. 8 1/2'
    B. 14'
    C. 15'
    D. 17'
    E. NG

28. How tall is a flagpole that makes a shadow of 20 feet when a yardstick makes a shadow   28.____
    of 1 foot 6 inches?

    A. 20 ft.   B. 40 ft.   C. 21 ft. 6 in.
    D. 60 ft.   E. NG

29. The figure shown at the right was once a regular prism, but some of the blocks have been taken away. How many are left?
    A. 23
    B. 24
    C. 32
    D. 36
    E. NG

29.____

30. A mixture formula reads, *Use 1/2 oz. per pint of water.* A pound will make how many gallons?

    A. 1   B. 2   C. 4   D. 8   E. NG

30.____

31. If all of x is part of y, and part of y is all of z, you know that

    A. all of x is z
    C. some of x is z
    E. x must equal 2 of y
    B. y is all of x and all of z
    D. none of z is part of x

31.____

32. How many different triangles are there in the figure shown at the right? Some of them overlap.
    A. 4
    B. 5
    C. 6
    D. 7
    E. NG

32.____

33. The amount of $1.00 at 4% interest compounded annually for 5 years is $1.2167. What would be the amount for $50.00 at 4% for 5 years?

    A. $52.00   B. $60.00   C. $60.20   D. $60.84   E. $68.35

33.____

34. A house that cost $20,000 is rented for $150 a month. Taxes, depreciation, and other costs amount to $600 for a year.
    What percent does the investment net for the year?

    A. 6   B. 4 1/2   C. 5   D. 4   E. NG

34.____

35. Jim tossed a coin 7 times. It came up heads twice.
    What are the chances that the next toss will be heads?

    A. 1 in 2   B. 5 in 8   C. 3 in 7   D. 1 in 8   E. NG

35.____

KEY (CORRECT ANSWERS)

1.	C	11.	D	21.	B	31.	B
2.	B	12.	A	22.	B	32.	D
3.	C	13.	A	23.	D	33.	D
4.	B	14.	A	24.	B	34.	E
5.	A	15.	E	25.	B	35.	A
6.	D	16.	D	26.	A		
7.	E	17.	B	27.	E		
8.	D	18.	C	28.	B		
9.	A	19.	D	29.	D		
10.	C	20.	C	30.	C		

———

SOLUTIONS TO PROBLEMS

1. Volume = (2")(3")(8") = 48 cu.in.

2. Difference in price = (.09)(12/2) -.49 = .05

3. In September, he spent $24 but only earned $4.

4. Total earnings = $26 + $18 + $16 + $4 + $8 = $72, whereas total spending = $8 + $4 + $22 + $24 + $14 = $72. He broke even.

5. In June, Tom saved $26 - $8 = $18, which was highest.

6. (40)(8) = 320 miles

7. (.25)(24/3) = $2.00

8. 6:15 P.M. - 7 1/2 hrs. = 10:45 A.M.

9. $60 \div \dfrac{1}{3}$ = 180 trailers

10. $\dfrac{40}{6} = 1$ in for $6\dfrac{2}{3}$ mi. $= 1\dfrac{1}{2}$ in. for 10 mi.

11. Total cost ÷ number of shares = cost per share

12. Sleep = 100% - 20% - 8% - 7% - 25% - 7% = 33%

13. Hours in school = (.25)(24) = 6

14. Nancy sold 30 boxes, which is 3 times as many as Betty sold.

15. Sue sold 25 boxes, which is 5 more than Ruth sold.

16. Betty sold 10 boxes.

17. $2000 + (12)($50) = $2600

18. $3740 - ($35)(48) = $2060

19. To find Father's monthly earnings, subtract Mother's salary from the sum of both, then divide by 12.

20. Circumference = $(\pi)(7") \approx (3\dfrac{1}{7})(7") = 22$ in

21. $(25+15+10+30+25)/5 = 105 \div 5 = 21$

22. Median = 3rd value from lowest to highest = 50 sec.
    (Tines are 40", 45", 50", 1'15", 1'30")

23. Rates per problem are as follows:
Larry: 75 sec/25 = 3 sec; Meg: 45 sec/15 = 3 sec.
Joe: 40 sec/10 = 4 sec; Sue: 90 sec/30 = 3 sec.
Bill: 50 sec/25 = 2 sec; so, Bill is fastest.

24. $30 \div 1.5 = 20$ Then, $(20)(.40) - (30)(.15) = \$3.50$

25. $(\$1.50)(4) = \$6.00$ rental cost per year. Then $\$30 \div \$6 = 5$ years.

26. Total cost = $(.05)(15) + (.05)(15) + (.05)(32) = \$3.10$

27. Diagonal = $\sqrt{5^2 + 12^2} = \sqrt{169} = 13$ ft.

28. Let x = height of flagpole. $\dfrac{3}{1\frac{1}{2}} = \dfrac{x}{20}$, $1\frac{1}{2}x = 60$, x = 40 ft.

29. 1st layer: 15 blocks; 2nd layer: 10 blocks; 3rd layer: 8 blocks; 4th layer: 3 blocks. Total = 36 blocks.

30. 1 lb. $\div \dfrac{1}{2}$ oz $= 32$. Then, 32 pints = $\dfrac{32}{8} = 4$ gallons.

31. There are 3 possible diagrams:

32. 1 large triangle, 4 separate smaller triangles, 2 "half" triangles. Total of 7 triangles. There are ACE, BCD, ABD, ADF, FDE, ACD, ADE.

33. $(50)(\$1.2167) = \$60.835 \approx 60.84$

34. $(\$150)(12) = \$1800$. Then, $\dfrac{\$1800}{\$20,600} \approx 8.7\%$

35. Regardless of the results of previous tosses, the probability that the next toss is heads = 1/2 = 1 in 2.

EXAMINATION SECTION
TEST 1

DIRECTIONS: Each question or incomplete statement is followed by several suggested answers or completions. Select the one that BEST answers the question or completes the statement. *PRINT THE LETTER OF THE CORRECT ANSWER IN THE SPACE AT THE RIGHT.*

1. Our number system has a base of   1._____

    A. 2   B. 5   C. 10   D. 60

2. To find the average weight of the football team,   2._____

    A. add and divide
    B. multiply
    C. add
    D. divide the weight of each player

3. The thermometer used to measure the temperature of a school is called   3._____

    A. Centigrade   B. Fahrenheit
    C. fever thermometer   D. gauge

4. The value of a fraction is changed when the same number is _____ to both numerator   4._____
and denominator.

    A. added
    B. divided
    C. multiplied
    D. reduced to both terms of the fraction

5. Stores buy their merchandise from firms called   5._____

    A. commissioners   B. retail firms
    C. factories   D. wholesale firms

6. The amount of money you borrow is called the   6._____

    A. amount   B. discount
    C. principal   D. bank discount

7. An angle of 75° is called a(n) _____ angle.   7._____

    A. acute   B. obtuse   C. straight   D. right

8. The rate of interest could be found by the formula   8._____

    A. $I = Prt$ B. $r = i/pt$ C. $r = Pt$ D. $I = P/Rt$

9. If three sides of one triangle are equal to the three sides of the other, the triangles are   9._____

    A. equilateral   B. right triangles
    C. scalene   D. congruent

10. A rectangular solid could be called a(n)   10.____

    A. plane   B. irregular figure
    C. polygon   D. prism

11. A written promise to repay the face of a loan is a   11.____

    A. refund   B. promissory note
    C. dividend   D. deposit

12. The ^{2} written above the s in the formula As^2 means   12.____

    A. 2s   B. s x s   C. s + s   D. s/2

13. Selling price includes cost plus profit plus   13.____

    A. expenses   B. profit   C. loss   D. net price

14. When numbers are used to express how many or how much of units of measure, they   14.____
are called

    A. digits   B. denominate numbers
    C. integers   D. whole numbers

15. The square of a number is that number multiplied by   15.____

    A. two   B. twice the number
    C. four   D. itself

16. When the merchant permits the customer to make a down payment and make regular   16.____
payments on an article, this form of payment is called

    A. dues   B. rent
    C. installment buying   D. utility payments

17. Circles that have a common center and different radii are _____ circles.   17.____

    A. equal   B. center   C. congruent   D. concentric

18. The United States standard of measure of length is the   18.____

    A. base 10   B. meter
    C. English system   D. metric system

19. If you put money to work for you, the income you receive is called   19.____

    A. income taxes   B. interest
    C. bank discount   D. sales tax

20. A fraction whose numerator is a fraction and denominator is an integer is a _____ frac-   20.____
tion.

    A. common   B. decimal   C. improper   D. complex

KEY (CORRECT ANSWERS)

1.	C	11.	B
2.	A	12.	B
3.	B	13.	A
4.	A	14.	B
5.	D	15.	D
6.	C	16.	C
7.	A	17.	D
8.	B	18.	C
9.	D	19.	B
10.	D	20.	D

SOLUTIONS TO PROBLEMS

1. 10 is the base of our number system. Ex: $456 = (4)(10^2) + (5)(10) + 6$.

2. To find average weight, add and divide.

3. Fahrenheit degrees would be used for schools.

4. A fraction will change when the same number is added to both numerator and denominator. Ex: Add 5 to both parts of 2/3 to get 7/8, and 7/8 ≠ 2/3.

5. Stores buy merchandise from wholesale firms.

6. Principal = amount of money borrowed.

7. 75° is an acute angle since it is less than 90°.

8. R = I/(PT) shows rate in terms of interest, principal, and time.

9. If 3 sides of one triangle match 3 sides of a second triangle, they are congruent (SSS).

10. A rectangular solid is a special kind of prism.

11. Promissory note = written promise to repay a loan.

12. $s^2 = s \times s$

13. Selling price includes cost, profit, and expenses.

14. Denominate numbers express units of measure. Ex: 8 gallons.

15. Square of any number = that number times itself. Ex: $4^2 = 4 \times 4 = 16$

16. Installment buying = down payment + regular payments Ex: $1000 down payment + $300 payment per month for 2 years.

17. Concentric circles have a common center but different radii. Diagram appears as:

18. The English system is the U.S. standard measure of length. This includes inches, feet, yards, miles, etc.

19. Interest = income received when money is put to work (invested).

20. A complex fraction would contain a fraction within its numerator, denominator, or both.

$$\text{Ex 1}: \frac{\frac{1}{2}}{\frac{1}{3}} = \frac{1}{2} \cdot \frac{3}{1} = \frac{3}{2}$$

$$\text{Ex 2}: \frac{1/2}{3} = \frac{1}{2} \cdot \frac{1}{3} = \frac{1}{6}$$

$$\text{Ex 3}: \frac{\frac{1}{2}}{\frac{2}{3}} = \frac{1}{2} \cdot \frac{3}{2} = \frac{3}{2}$$

_____

TEST 2

DIRECTIONS: Each question or incomplete statement is followed by several suggested answers or completions. Select the one that BEST answers the question or completes the statement. *PRINT THE LETTER OF THE CORRECT ANSWER IN THE SPACE AT THE RIGHT.*

1. Sally is going to Chicago for a visit. The bus fare is $27.85 one way or a round-trip ticket would be $51.56. How much can Sally save by buying a round-trip ticket rather than two one-way tickets?

   A. $4.20
   C. $4.14
   B. $2.07
   D. None of the above

   1.____

2. The Webster Junior High School collected $226.45 for Junior Red Cross and $420.55 for the Community Chest. There were 850 students in the school.
   To the NEAREST cent, what was the average contribution?

   A. $.76
   C. $1.00
   B. $.50
   D. None of the above

   2.____

3. Jack borrowed $57.50 from his father and agreed to pay it in twelve monthly payments of $5.00 each.
   How much interest did he pay?

   A. $2.50
   C. $7.50
   B. $3.50
   D. None of the above

   3.____

4. Joe's mother bought a roast weighing 6 3/4 lbs. at 89? a pound.
   How much change did she receive from a $10.00 bill?

   A. $3.99
   C. $6.01
   B. $5.01
   D. None of the above

   4.____

5. The Athletic Department paid $45 total tax on 1,000 tickets.
   How much tax was this per ticket?

   A. $.22
   C. 4.5 cents
   B. $.45
   D. None of the above

   5.____

6. Mary bought 4 1/2 yards of lace. She used 1 2/3 yards of it on a blouse.
   _____ yards of lace were left.

   A. 3 1/6
   C. 2 5/6
   B. 3 1/2
   D. None of the above

   6.____

7. The girls are going to make aprons for Junior Red Cross. The pattern calls for 3/4 yard of material for one apron. They will need _____ yards for 25 aprons.

   A. 33 1/3
   C. 20
   B. 18 3/4
   D. None of the above

   7.____

8. Which city on a world map of standard time zones would be NEAR the 75°W?

   A. Greenwich
   C. Calcutta
   B. Sydney
   D. None of the above

   8.____

9. John's father made a down payment on a car and has $1320 left to pay. He pays $55 9.____
each month.
It will take him _____ months to finish the car payments.

   A. 42   B. 24
   C. 18   D. None of the above

10. Pete bought a board 12 ft. 8 in. long from which he wants to make three shelves. Two of 10.____
the shelves are 2 ft. 8 in. long, and the third shelf is 1 ft. 6 in. long.
How long will the piece be that is left over?

   A. 5 ft. 8 in.   B. 5 ft. 10 in.
   C. 6 ft. 10 in.   D. None of the above

11. A factory worker received an increase of 15% in his hourly wages. His former wages 11.____
were $1.80 per hour.
How much a week did his wages INCREASE in a forty-hour week?

   A. $21.17   B. $8.00
   C. $10.80   D. None of the above

12. Find the installment price of a washing machine if the down payment is $39.90, the 12.____
monthly payments are $14.13 for twelve months, and the interest charge is $9.96.

   A. $179.52   B. $219.42
   C. $169.56   D. None of the above

13. How many hundreds in 18762? 13.____

   A. 7   B. 87
   C. 187   D. None of the above

14. The football team won 16 games and lost 4 games. What percent of the games played 14.____
did they win?

   A. 75%   B. 80%
   C. 40%   D. None of the above

15. The bakery boxed doughnuts one half dozen to a box. 15.____
They will have _____ full boxes if they fry 500 doughnuts.

   A. 41   B. 83
   C. 82   D. None of the above

16. Jane's parents burn fuel oil. They have used 180 gallons. The gauge indicates the tank is 16.___
5/8 full.
The tank holds _____ gallons.

   A. 255   B. 480
   C. 600   D. None of the above

17. _____ tiles, each a 9" square, could be laid in one width of a recreation room that is 25 17.___
feet long and 16 1/2 feet wide.

   A. 22   B. 149
   C. 51   D. None of the above

18. The outside diameter of a wheel on Bob's bicycle is 28 inches. The outside diameter of a wheel on his little brother's bicycle is 21 inches. After traveling a mile the little brother's wheel will make _____ revolutions more.   18._____

    A. 1080   B. 269.5
    C. 240   D. None of the above

19. Bill gets 17 3/4 miles per gallon.   19._____
At this rate, he should get _____ miles if he buys 5.6 gallons of gasoline.

    A. 317   B. 99.4
    C. 85   D. None of the above

20. The scale drawing of a house is 1 in. = 12 ft.   20._____
If a room is 33 feet long, a _____ inch line should be used on the blueprint to represent that distance.

    A. 2 3/4   B. 3.3
    C. 2.1   D. None of the above

21. A 2-inch gear makes 75 revolutions per minute.   21._____
A 3-inch gear makes _____ rpm at the same rate of speed.

    A. 12 1/2   B. 112 1/2
    C. 50   D. None of the above

22. What is the selling price of a radio that cost the dealer $36 and the margin is 40% of the selling price?   22._____

    A. $60   B. $45
    C. $50.40   D. None of the above

23. Mr. Jacks used 35 kwh.   23._____
If the charge is 8¢ a kwh for the first 20 kwh and 5¢ a kwh for the remainder, what was the TOTAL charge?

    A. $2.35   B. $3.35
    C. $4.55   D. None of the above

24. Druggists use a unit of measurement of weight called the grain. There are *approximately* 437.5 grains in an ounce. There are APPROXIMATELY _____ grains in a pound.   24._____

    A. 7000   B. 5252
    C. 73,400   D. None of the above

25. A gasoline tank is 16 ft. high and has a diameter of 14 ft.   25._____
The tank will hold _____ cubic feet of gasoline (use 22/7 for pi) to the NEAREST 10 cu.ft.

    A. 704   B. 784
    C. 2460   D. None of the above

KEY (CORRECT ANSWERS)

1.	C		11.	C
2.	A		12.	B
3.	A		13.	C
4.	A		14.	B
5.	C		15.	B
6.	C		16.	B
7.	B		17.	A
8.	D		18.	C
9.	B		19.	B
10.	B		20.	A

21.	C
22.	A
23.	A
24.	A
25.	C

SOLUTIONS TO PROBLEMS

1. Savings = ($27.85)(2) - $51.56 = $4.14

2. Average contribution = ($226.45 + $420.55) ÷ 850 = $647 ÷ 850 ≈ $.76

3. Interest = (12)($5.00) - $57.50 = $2.50

4. $10.00 - (6.75)(.89) = $3.99 change

5. $45 ÷ 1000 = .045 = 4.5 cents tax per ticket

6. 4 1/2 - 1 2/3 = 4 3/6 - 1 4/6 = 3 9/6 - 1 4/6 = 2 5/6 yds. left

7. (3/4)(25) = 18 3/4 yds. needed

8. Refer to world map. None is correct.

9. $1320 ÷ 55 = 24 months

10. 12'8" - 2'8" - 2'8" - 1'6" = 152" - 32" - 32" - 18" = 70" = 5'10"

11. Increase = ($1.80)(.15)(40) = $10.80 per week

12. $39.90 + ($14.13)(12) + $9.96 = $219.42 installment price

13. 18,762 ÷ 100 = 187 with remainder of 62. So, there are 187 hundreds in 18,762.

14. Percent won = 16/20 = 80%

15. 500 ÷ 6 = 83 1/3, which means 83 full boxes + 1/3 of a box

16. 180 gallons represents 3/8 of the entire tank. Thus, the tank's capacity = 180 ÷ 3/8 = 480 gallons.

17. 25' = 300" and 16 1/2' = 198". Now, 300 ÷ 9 = 33 1/3 and 198 ÷ 9 = 22. Then the number of tiles that could fit in 1 width = 22. (The actual number of tiles that could fit in the entire room = (22)(33) = 726)

18. 1 revolution of Bob's bicycle = $2\pi r = (2 \times \frac{22}{7} \times 14) = 88"$

    1 revolution of his brother's bicycle = $2\pi r = (2 \times \frac{22}{7} \times 10.5) = 66"$

    1 mile = 63,360"

    ∴ Bob's bicycle wheel will make (63,360/88) revs

    His brother's wheel will make (63,360/66) revs = 960

    ∴ His brother's wheel will make 240 revs more

19. $(17\frac{3}{4})$ (5.6) = (17.75)(5.6) = 99.4 miles

20. 33 ÷ 12 = 2 3/4 -inch line needed

21. Let x = rpm. 2/3 = x/75 . Solving, x = 50

    Note: Size of gear is inversely related to rpm.

22. Let x = selling price. Then, $36 = .60x. Solving, x = $60

23. Total charge = (.08)(20) + (.05)(15) = $2.35

24. (437.5)(16) = 7000 grains in a pound (approx.)

25. Volume = $(\pi)(7^2)(16) \approx 2460$ cu.ft.

———

ARITHMETICAL REASONING
EXAMINATION SECTION
TEST 1

DIRECTIONS: Each question or incomplete statement is followed by several suggested answers or completions. Select the one that BEST answers the question or completes the statement. *PRINT THE LETTER OF THE CORRECT ANSWER IN THE SPACE AT THE RIGHT.*

1. The initial mark-up in a store is 40%; mark-downs are 5%; shortages 1%; cash discounts 5%; alteration costs 5%; expenses 25%.
The maintained mark-up is

    A. 34%   B. 39%   C. 36.4%   D. 30%

1.____

2. A buyer of TV sets wishes to maintain a mark-up of 37 1/2% after all mark-downs are taken. Of 25 sets costing $150 each, he sells 20 at $265.
How much can he mark-down the remaining 5 sets and still realize his mark-up objective?

    A. $166   B. $150   C. $140   D. $125

2.____

3. An article originally selling for $12 and costing $8 was marked down to $10. Assuming the same markup,
what is the present market value of its cost?

    A. $6.68   B. $8.00   C. $5.67   D. $6.86

3.____

4. What is the *on* percentage of trade discounts of 20% and 10%?

    A. 70   B. 85   C. 72   D. 80

4.____

5. Canadian cost of a sweater is $40. Packing and labor cost $5.00; ad valorem duty, 40%; specific duty, 65¢; rate of exchange, .9091.
What is the duty in American currency?

    A. $16.96   B. $16.36   C. $18.00   D. $18.60

5.____

6. A bolt of cloth measures 40 yards. The following yardages are sold: 4 1/2, 5 3/4, 6 7/8.
How many yards are left?

    A. 23 7/8   B. 22 1/2   C. 22 7/8   D. 24 3/8

6.____

7. A shirt manufacturer has 76 1/2 yards of broadcloth to be used for shirts.
If each shirt takes 2 1/2 yards, how many shirts can he make?

    A. 38   B. 30   C. 19   D. 31

7.____

8. Subtract 1.003 from 24.5.

    A. 24.003   B. 12.42   C. 23.2   D. 23.497

8.____

9. A store carries a stock amounting to $265,830.25. Cash discounts, on the average, amount to 5 1/4%.
   How much are the cash discounts?

   A. $13,956.09   B. $1,395.61
   C. $139.56   D. $1.39

9.____

10. If the sales in a department totaled $67,507.50 and the average sale was $22.50, how many transactions were there?

   A. 3,000   B. 300   C. 30,000   D. 30

10.____

11. A department store reports a decrease in sales of 5.5% for this year.
    If this year's sales are $275,825,000, last year's sales were

   A. $291,878,000   B. $290,995,000
   C. $260,655,000   D. $290,788,000

11.____

12. For the current year, the sales volume in a store was $50,000,000. Other income amounted to $1,500,000, Operating expenses were $10,000,000; cost of goods sold, $37,500,000.
    What is the percent of net profit based on retail?

   A. 10   B. 8   C. 50   D. 13

12.____

13. If this year's sales show an increase of 300% over last year, this year's sales are how many times last year's sales?

   A. 3   B. 1 1/3   C. 4   D. 1/4

13.____

14. Net sales in a shop amounted to $374,000; returns were 10%; allowances, 5%.
    What were the gross sales?

   A. $430,100   B. $415,000   C. $411,400   D. $440,000

14.____

15. If the average sale in a store is expected to rise 5% over last year, and the number of transactions increases 3%, what percentage of increase in dollar sales volume should be planned?

   A. 8   B. 4   C. 8.15   D. 8.51

15.____

16. The billed cost on an invoice is $300; freight charges, $10; cash discount, 2%; the retail value of the merchandise is $525.
    The mark-up percent on retail is

   A. 40.9   B. 42   C. 69   D. 69.5

16.____

17. A hat costing $30.00 is to be given a mark-up of 45% on retail.
    The retail should be

   A. $43.50   B. $46.40   C. $55.40   D. $54.50

17.____

18. Retail price $40 per unit; mark-up 40% of retail; transportation charge $1 per unit.
    Find billed cost that store can pay.

   A. $23   B. $24   C. $23.75   D. $24.75

18.____

19. A buyer plans to spend $17,000 at retail for merchandise at a mark-up of 34%. He finds a special value at $3,000 that he can sell for $6,000.
What mark-up percentage does he need on the balance of his purchases in order to achieve his planned 34%?

    A. 35   B. 19.9   C. 15   D. 22.5

19.____

20. A store has a gross margin of 40% and reductions of 13%. Cash discount on purchases are not credited to the department. There are no alteration costs.
What is the initial mark-up?

    A. 46%   B. 53%   C. 27%   D. 26%

20.____

21. A dress is to retail for $35 with a mark-up of 40% of retail.
The cost of the dress to the retailer was

    A. $25   B. $21   C. $14   D. $20

21.____

22. The cost is $1.20 and the desired gross profit is 40% of retail.
The retail price should be

    A. $1.60   B. $1.68   C. $2.00   D. $2.40

22.____

23. The realized mark-up on a TV set is $50. The mark-up is 25% of retail.
The cost of the TV set to the retailer was

    A. $200   B. $125   C. $100   D. $150

23.____

24. Farnum, a salesman, earns $9.60 per hour for 40 hours a week, with time and a half for all hours over 40 per week. Last week, his total earnings were $470.40.
How many hours did he work last week?

    A. 46   B. 49   C. 47   D. 48

24.____

25. Dane & Clarke, partners, share profits in a 5:3 ratio. Dane's share of the profit for this year was $12,000 more than Clarke's share.
Clarke's share of the net profit was

    A. $30,000   B. $48,000   C. $36,000   D. $18,000

25.____

—————

KEY (CORRECT ANSWERS)

1.	C	11.	A
2.	D	12.	B
3.	A	13.	C
4.	C	14.	D
5.	A	15.	C
6.	C	16.	A
7.	B	17.	D
8.	D	18.	A
9.	A	19.	B
10.	A	20.	A

21.	B
22.	C
23.	D
24.	A
25.	D

———

SOLUTIONS TO PROBLEMS

1. 5 + 5 – 1 = 9%. Then, (40%)(.91) = 36.4%.

2. (25)($150) = $3750 and $3750 .625 = $6000 total selling price of all sets. $6000 - (20)($265) = $700; 700 5 = $140 selling price for each of the last 5 sets. Markdown amount = $265 -$140 = $125

3. When the article's original selling price was $12, its cost was $8.00. If the article's original selling price were to be $10, it would cost $(8.00/12.00 x 10.00) = $6.67

4. Resulting percentage = (1-.20)(1-.10) = .72 = 72%

5. ($45)(.40) = $18, 18 + .65 = $18.65. Then, ($18.65)(.9091) = $16.95, closest to $16.96 in American currency.

6. 40 - 4 1/2 - 5 3/4 - 6 7/8 = 22 7/8 yds.

7. 76 1/2 ÷ 2 1/2 = 30.6, rounded down to 30 shirts

8. 24.5 - 1.003 = 23.497

9. ($265,830.25)(.0525) = $13,956.09

10. $67,507.50 $22.50 = 3000 transactions

11. $275,825,000 .945 = $291,878,000

12. $50,000,000 + $1,500,000 - $10,000,000 - $37,500,000 = $4,000,000 Then, $4,000,000 $50,000,000 = .08 = 8%

13. An increase of 300% over x = 4x, so sales are 4 times as large.

14. Gross sales = $374,000 .85 = $440,000

15. (1.05)(1.03) = 1.0815, which represents an 8.15% increase in dollar sales volume

16. $525 - $310 = $215; then, $215/$525 = 40.9%

17. $30 will represent 55% of retail amount. Thus, retail will be $30 .55 = $54.50

18. ($40)(.60) - $1 = $23

19. ($17,000)(1.34) = $22,780. Then, $22,780 - $6000 = $16,780. Also, $17,000 - $3,000 = $14,000. Finally, ($16,780 - $14,000) ÷ $14,000 ≈ 19.9%

20. Let x = markup percent. Then, x-40/x = .13 Solving, x = 46

21. Cost = ($35)(.60) = $21

22. Let x = retail price. Then, $1.20 = .60x. Solving, x = $2.00

23. $50 = 25% of retail, so retail = $200. Thus, cost = $200 - $50 = $150

24. Let x = overtime hours. Then, ($9.60)(40) + $14.40x = $470.40 Solving, x = 6. Total hours worked = 46

25. 5x - 3x - $12,000. So, x = $6000. Clarke's share = (3)($6000) = $18,000

———

TEST 2

DIRECTIONS: Each question or incomplete statement is followed by several suggested answers or completions. Select the one that BEST answers the question or completes the statement. *PRINT THE LETTER OF THE CORRECT ANSWER IN THE SPACE AT THE RIGHT.*

1. Assume that you require 77 dozen felt practice golf balls. Which of the following repre-   1.____
sents the LOWEST bid for these balls?

    A. 41¢ per half-dozen less a 3% discount
    B. 83¢ per dozen less a 7 1/2% discount
    C. 85¢ per dozen less a 10% discount
    D. $65.00 less a series discount of 3%, 2%

2. Assume that you require 1,944 rulers, packed 12 to the box, 18 boxes to the carton.   2.____
Which of the following represents the LOWEST bid for these rulers?

    A. 5 1/2¢ per ruler
    B. 6¢ for the first 750 rulers; 5 1/2¢ for the next 750 rulers; 4 1/2¢ for every ruler there-
after
    C. $11.85 per carton
    D. $110 less series discounts of 2%, 1%

3. Assume that you require 20 cartons of colored raffia, cellophane wrapped in one lb.   3.____
packages, 50 packages to the carton.
Which of the following represents the LOWEST bid for the raffia?

    A. 8¢ per lb.; 15¢ per carton packing charge; 20¢ per carton delivery charge
    B. 9¢ per lb. less a 3% discount
    C. 10¢ per lb. for the first 150 lbs.; 9¢ per lb. for the next 200 lbs.; 80 for each lb. there-
after
    D. $83.50 less a 4 1/2% discount

4. Assume that you require 50 yards of table felt, 48" wide, and 12 yards of table felt, 72"   4.____
wide.
Which of the following represents the LOWEST bid for this felt?

    A. 32¢ per yard (48" wide), 40¢ per yard (72" wide)
    B. 34¢ per yard (48" wide), 43¢ per yard (72" wide); series discounts of 5%, 3%
    C. 360 per yard (48" wide), 41¢ per yard (72" wide); 8% discount, packing charge 75¢
    D. $23.00 for the order, 9% discount, packing charge 50¢

5. If the cost of 3 erasers is 5¢, the cost of 2 1/2 dozen erasers is   5.____

    A. 18¢   B. 37 1/2¢   C. 50¢   D. 31 1/2¢

6. A circle graph of a budget shows the expenditure of 26.2% for housing, 28.4% for food,   6.____
12% for clothing, 12.7% for taxes, and the balance for miscellaneous items.
The percent for miscellaneous items is

    A. 31.5   B. 79.3   C. 20.7   D. 68.5

7. The cost of a broadloom rug measuring 4 feet by 6 feet, at $6.30 per square yard, is

    A. $16.80   B. $50.40   C. $37.60   D. $21.00

7.____

8. The number of tiles each measuring 2 inches by 3 inches needed for a wall 3 feet high and 5 feet long is

    A. 180   B. 30   C. 360   D. 60

8.____

9. Assume that you require 4 tons of fertilizer. The fertilizer is packed in 100 pound bags. Which of the following represents the LOWEST bid for the fertilizer?

    A. 6¢ per pound
    B. $5.50 per bag
    C. $7.00 for each of the first 30 bags; $5.00 for each bag thereafter
    D. $500.00 less 3 1/2% discount

9.____

10. Assume pencils are packed 5 gross to the case. A buyer requires 3,800 pencils each for three departments and 2,700 pencils for another department. Assume that the vendor will ship unbroken cases only directly to each department.
How many cases should he buy?

    A. 21   B. 22   C. 48   D. 49

10.____

11. Assume that a buyer had to purchase 40,000 lbs. of salt. Which one of the following bids should he accept, assuming quality, service, and delivery terms are all the same?

    A. 1¢ per pound, 2%-30 days
    B. 99¢ per 100 lbs., 1%-30 days
    C. $19 per ton, 1%-30 days
    D. $18 per ton, net-30 days

11.____

12. Which one of the following four bids represents the BEST value, assuming delivery costs amount to $100?

    A. $1,000 f.o.b. buyer, less 2%-10 days
    B. $900 f.o.b. seller, less 2%-10 days
    C. $975 delivered, net cash 30 days
    D. $990 f.o.b. buyer, less 1%-10 days

12.____

13. Suppose that four suppliers make the following offers to sell 2,000 units of a particular commodity.
Which one is the MOST advan12tageous proposal?

    A. $10 list, less 40% and 5%
    B. $5 cost, plus 20% to cover overhead and profit
    C. $10 list, less 20% and 20%
    D. $5 cost, plus 10% overhead and 10% for profit

13.____

14. Suppose that you purchase 100 units of an item at a list of $1 per unit less 40% and 10%, and less 2% if paid within 10 days.
If payment is made within the 10-day limit, the amount of the payment should be

    A. $52.92   B. $54.00   C. $58.80   D. $60.00

14.____

15. Assume that the 1987 cost of living factor was 100 and that a certain product was selling   15.____
that year for $5 per unit. Assume further that at the present time the cost of living factor is
150.
If the selling price of the product increased 10% more than the cost of living during this
period, at the present time the product would be selling for ____ per unit.

    A. $8.25   B. $10.50   C. $16.50   D. $7.75

16. A certain food is sold in 4 ounce cans at 10 for $1.00 and in 1 pound cans at 3 for $1.00.   16.____
The savings in price per ounce by purchasing the food in the larger can is ____ cents/
ounce.

    A. .53   B. .35   C. .42   D. .68

17. After an article is discounted at 25%, it sells for $375. The ORIGINAL price of the article   17.____
was

    A. $93.75   B. $350   C. $375   D. $500

18. Assume that you require 1,440 pencils, packed 12 to the box, 24 boxes to the carton.   18.____
Which of the following represents the LOWEST bid for these pencils?

    A. 2¢ per pencil
    B. $6.50 per carton
    C. 27¢ per box less a 4% discount
    D. $40 less a 3% discount

19. If erasers cost 8¢ each for the first 250, 70 each for the next 250, and 5¢ for every eraser   19.____
thereafter, how many erasers may be purchased for $50?

    A. 600   B. 750   C. 850   D. 1,000

20. Assume that a buyer saves $14 on the purchase of an item that is discounted at 25%.   20.____
The amount of money that the buyer must pay for the item is

    A. $42   B. $52   C. $54   D. $56

Questions 21-24.

DIRECTIONS: Questions 21 through 24 are to be answered on the basis of the following
method of obtaining a reorder point: multiply the monthly rate of consumption
by the lead time (in months) and add the minimum balance.

21. If the lead time is one-half month, the minimum balance is 6 units, and the monthly rate   21.____
of consumption is 4 units, then the reorder point is ____ units.

    A. 4   B. 6   C. 8   D. 12

22. If the reorder point is 25 units, the lead time is 3 months, and the minimum balance is 10   22.____
units, then the average monthly rate of consumption is ____ units.

    A. 3   B. 5   C. 6   D. 10

23. If the reorder point is 400 units, the lead time is 2 months, and the monthly rate of con-   23.____
sumption is 150 units, then the minimum balance is ____ units.

    A. 50   B. 100   C. 150   D. 200

24. If the reorder point is 75 units, the monthly rate of consumption is 60 units, and the mini-   24.____
mum balance is 45 units, then the lead time is ____month(s).

   A. 1/2   B. 1   C. 2   D. 4

25. A purchasing office has 4,992 special requisitions to be processed. Working alone,   25.____
Buyer A could process these in 30 days; working alone, Buyer B could process these in
40 days; working alone, Buyer C could process these in 60 days.
The LEAST number of days in which Buyers A, B, and C working together can process
these 4,992 special requisitions is APPROXIMATELY____ days.

   A. 14   B. 20   C. 34   D. 45

KEY (CORRECT ANSWERS)

1.	C	11.	D
2.	B	12.	C
3.	D	13.	A
4.	B	14.	A
5.	C	15.	A
6.	C	16.	C
7.	A	17.	D
8.	C	18.	A
9.	B	19.	B
10.	B	20.	A

21.	C
22.	B
23.	B
24.	A
25.	A

SOLUTIONS TO PROBLEMS

1. Bid A = (.82)(77)(.97) $\approx$ $61.25;
   Bid B = (.83)(77)(.925) $\approx$ $59.12
   Bid C = (.85)(77)(.90) $\approx$ $58.91;
   Bid D = ($65.00)(.97)(.98) $\approx$ $61.79 Thus, Bid C is lowest.

2. Bid A = (.055)(1944) = $106.92;
   Bid B = (.06)(750)+(.055)(750) + (.045)(444) = $106.23;
   Bid C = ($11.85)(9) = $106.65;
   Bid D = ($110)(.98)(.99) $\approx$ $106.72. Thus, Bid B is lowest.

3. Bid A = (.08)(1000) + (.15)(20) + (.20)(20) = $87.00
   Bid B = (.09)(1000)(.97) = $87.30
   Bid C = (.10)(150) + (.09)(200) + (.08)(650) = $85.00
   Bid D = ($83.50)(.955) $\approx$ $79.74
   Thus, Bid D is lowest.

4. Bid A = (.32)(50)+(.40)(12) = $20.80
   Bid B = (.34)(50)+(.43)(12) = $22.16; so ($22.16)(.95)(.97) $\approx$ $20.42
   Bid C = (.36)(50)+(.41)(12) = $22.92; so ($22.92)(.92)+.75 $\approx$ $21.84
   Bid D = ($23.00)(.91)+.50 = $21.43
   Bid B is lowest.

5. (2 1/2)(12) = 30 erasers, which will cost (.05)(10) = 50¢

6. 100 - 26.2 - 28.4 - 12 - 12.7 = 20.7% for miscellaneous items

7. 24 ÷ 9 = 2 2/3 sq.yds. Then, ($6.30)(2 2/3) = $16.80

8. 3' 2" = 18; 5' 3" = 20. Thus, (18)(20) = 360 tiles

9. Bid A = (.06)(8000) = $480
   Bid B = ($5.50)(80) = $440
   Bid C = ($7.00)(30)+($5.00)(50) = $460 Bid D - ($500)(.965) = $482.50 Thus,
   Bid B is lowest.

10. 5 gross = 5(144) = 720; 3800 will be 6 unbroken cases x 3 = 18
    2700 will be 4 unbroken cases = 4
    ——
    22

11. Bid A = (.01)(40,000)(.98) = $392.00
    Bid B = (.99)(400)(.99) = $392.04
    Bid C = ($19)(20)(.99) = $376.20
    Bid D = ($18)(20) = $360.00
    Bid D is lowest.

12. A. 1,000 - 2% = 980
    B. 900 + 100 - 2% = 980

C. 975
D. 990 - 9.90 = 980.10
C is best value

13. Proposal A: ($10)(.60)(.95) = $5.70
Proposal B: $5 + ($5)(.20) = $6.00
Proposal C: ($10) (.80)(.80) = $6.40
Proposal D: $5 + (.20)($5) = $6.00
Proposal A is lowest.

14. Payment = ($100)(.60)(.90)(.98) = $52.92

15. Present cost = ($5)(1.50)(1.10) = $8.25

16. 40 ounces for $1.00 in smaller cans means 2.5 cents per ounce. For the larger cans, (3)(16) = 48 ounces for $1.00, which means $2.08\overline{3}$ cents per ounce. The savings is approximately .42 cents per ounce.

17. Original price = $375 ÷ .75 = $500

18. Bid A = (1440)(.02) = $28.80
Bid B = (1440 ÷ 288)($6.50) = $32.50
Bid C = [(144 ÷ 12)(.27)] [.96] = $31.10
Bid D = ($40)(.97) = $38.80
Bid A is lowest.

19. 250 erasers cost (250)(.08) = $20
500 erasers cost $20 + (250)(.07) = $37.50
The number of additional erasers = ($50 - $37.50) ÷ .05 = 250
Total number of erasers = 750

20. $14 ÷ .25 = $56. Then, $56 - $14 = $42

21. (4)(.5) +6 = 8 units

22. Let x = monthly rate. Then, (x)(3) + 10 = 25. Solving, x = 5 units

23. Let x = minimum balance. (150)(2) + x = 400. Solving, x = 100 units

24. Let x = lead time. (60)(x) + 45 = 75. Solving, x = 1/2 month

25. Buyer A does 4992 ÷ 30 ≈ 166 per day
Buyer B does 4992 ÷ 40 ≈ 125 per day
Buyer C does 4992 ÷ 60 ≈ 83 per day
Working together, approximately 374 requisitions are done per day. Finally, 4992 ÷ 374 ≈ 13, closest to 14 in selections.

CLERICAL ABILITIES TEST

EXAMINATION SECTION
TEST 1

DIRECTIONS: Each question or incomplete statement is followed by several suggested answers or completions. Select the one that *BEST* answers the question or completes the statement. *PRINT THE LETTER OF THE CORRECT ANSWER IN THE SPACE AT THE RIGHT.*

Questions 1-10.

DIRECTIONS: Questions 1 through 10 consist of lines of names, dates and numbers. For each question, you are to choose the option (A, B, C, or D) in Column II which *EXACTLY* matches the information in Column I. *PRINT THE LETTER OF THE CORRECT ANSWER IN THE SPACE AT THE RIGHT.*

SAMPLE QUESTION

Column I	Column II		
Schneider 11/16/75 581932	A. Schneider	11/16/75	518932
	B. Schneider	11/16/75	581932
	C. Schnieder	11/16/75	581932
	D. Shnieder	11/16/75	518932

The correct answer is B. Only option B shows the name, date and number exactly as they are in Column I. Option A has a mistake in the number. Option C has a mistake in the name. Option D has a mistake in the name and in the number. Now answer Questions 1 through 10 in the same manner.

	Column I		Column II	
1.	Johnston 12/26/74 659251	A.	Johnson 12/23/74 659251	1._____
		B.	Johston 12/26/74 659251	
		C.	Johnston 12/26/74 695251	
		D.	Johnston 12/26/74 659251	
2.	Allison 1/26/75 9939256	A.	Allison 1/26/75 9939256	2._____
		B.	Alisson 1/26/75 9939256	
		C.	Allison 1/26/76 9399256	
		D.	Allison 1/26/75 9993256	
3.	Farrell 2/12/75 361251	A.	Farell 2/21/75 361251	3._____
		B.	Farrell 2/12/75 361251	
		C.	Farrell 2/21/75 361251	
		D.	Farrell 2/12/75 361151	
4.	Guerrero 4/28/72 105689	A.	Guererro 4/28/72 105689	4._____
		B.	Guererro 4/28/72 105986	
		C.	Guerrero 4/28/72 105869	
		D.	Guerrero 4/28/72 105689	

5. McDonnell 6/05/73 478215

    A. McDonnell 6/15/73 478215   5.___
    B. McDonnell 6/05/73 478215
    C. McDonnell 6/05/73 472815
    D. MacDonell 6/05/73 478215

6. Shepard 3/31/71 075421

    A. Sheperd 3/31/71 075421   6.___
    B. Shepard 3/13/71 075421
    C. Shepard 3/31/71 075421
    D. Shepard 3/13/71 075241

7. Russell 4/01/69 031429

    A. Russell 4/01/69 031429   7.___
    B. Russell 4/10/69 034129
    C. Russell 4/10/69 031429
    D. Russell 4/01/69 034129

8. Phillips 10/16/68 961042

    A. Philipps 10/16/68 961042   8.___
    B. Phillips 10/16/68 960142
    C. Phillips 10/16/68 961042
    D. Philipps 10/16/68 916042

9. Campbell 11/21/72 624856

    A. Campbell 11/21/72 624856   9.___
    B. Campbell 11/21/72 624586
    C. Campbell 11/21/72 624686
    D. Campbel 11/21/72 624856

10. Patterson 9/18/71 76199176

    A. Patterson 9/18/72 76191976   10.___
    B. Patterson 9/18/71 76199176
    C. Patterson 9/18/72 76199176
    D. Patterson 9/18/71 76919176

Questions 11-15.

DIRECTIONS: Questions 11 through 15 consist of groups of numbers and letters which you are to compare. For each question, you are to choose the option (A, B, C, or D) in Column II which *EXACTLY* matches the group of numbers and letters given in Column I.

SAMPLE QUESTION

Column I
B92466

Column II
A. B92644
B. B94266
C. A92466
D. B92466

The correct answer is D. Only option D in Column II shows the group of numbers and letters *EXACTLY* as it appears in Column I. Now answer Questions 11 through 15 in the same manner.

Column I	Column II
11. 925AC5	A. 952CA5
	B. 925AC5
	C. 952AC5
	D. 925CA6

12.   Y006925

           A. Y060925
           B. Y006295
           C. Y006529
           D. Y006925

13.   J236956

           A. J236956
           B. J326965
           C. J239656
           D. J932656

14.   AB6952

           A. AB6952
           B. AB9625
           C. AB9652
           D. AB6925

15.   X259361

           A. X529361
           B. X259631
           C. X523961
           D. X259361

Questions 16-25.

DIRECTIONS: Each of Questions 16 through 25 consists of three lines of code letters and three lines of numbers. The numbers on each line should correspond with the code letters on the same line in accordance with the table below.

Code Letter	S	V	W	A	Q	M	X	E	G	K
Corresponding Number	0	1	2	3	4	5	6	7	8	9

On some of the lines, an error exists in the coding. Compare the letters and numbers in each question carefully. If you find an error or errors on:

> only *one* of the lines in the question, mark your answer A;
> any *two* lines in the question, mark your answer B;
> all *three* lines in the question, mark your answer C;
> *none* of the lines in the question, mark your answer D.

SAMPLE QUESTION

    WQGKSXG   2489068
    XEKVQMA   6591453
    KMAESXV   9527061

In the above example, the first line is correct since each code letter listed has the correct corresponding number. On the second line, an error exists because code letter E should have the number 7 instead of the number 5. On the third line an error exists because the code letter A should have the number 3 instead of the number 2. Since there are errors in two of the three lines, the correct answer is B. Now answer Questions 16 through 25 in the same manner.

16.   SWQEKGA   0247983   16._____
      KEAVSXM   9731065
      SSAXGKQ   0036894

17.   QAMKMVS   4259510   17._____
      MGGEASX   5897306
      KSWMKWS   9125920

18.	WKXQWVE	2964217	18.___
	QKXXQVA	4966413	
	AWMXGVS	3253810	

19.	GMMKASE	8559307	19.___
	AWVSKSW	3210902	
	QAVSVGK	4310189	

20.	XGKQSMK	6894049	20.___
	QSVKEAS	4019730	
	GSMXKMV	8057951	

21.	AEKMWSG	3195208	21.___
	MKQSVQK	5940149	
	XGQAEVW	6843712	

22.	XGMKAVS	6858310	22.___
	SKMAWEQ	0953174	
	GVMEQSA	8167403	

23.	VQSKAVE	1489317	23.___
	WQGKAEM	2489375	
	MEGKAWQ	5689324	

24.	XMQVSKG	6541098	24.___
	QMEKEWS	4579720	
	KMEVKGA	9571983	

25.	GKVAMEW	8912572	25.___
	AXMVKAE	3651937	
	KWAGMAV	9238531	

Questions 26-35.

DIRECTIONS: Each of Questions 26 through 35 consists of a column of figures. For each question, add the column of figures and choose the correct answer from the four choices given.

26. 5,665.43
2,356.69
6,447.24
7,239.65

  A. 20,698.01   B. 21,709.01
  C. 21,718.01   D. 22,609.01

26.___

27. 817,209.55
264,354.29
82,368.76
849,964.89

  A. 1,893,997.49   B. 1,989,988.39
  C. 2,009,077.39   D. 2,013,897,49

27.___

28. 156,366.89
249,973.23
823,229.49
56,869.45

    A. 1,286,439.06   B. 1,287,521.06
    C. 1,297,539.06   D. 1,296,421.06

28.____

29. 23,422.15
149,696.24
238,377.53
86,289.79
505,544.63

    A. 989,229.34   B. 999,879.34
    C. 1,003,330.34   D. 1,023,329.34

29.____

30. 2,468,926.70
656,842.28
49,723.15
832,369.59

    A. 3,218,061.72   B. 3,808,092.72
    C. 4,007,861.72   D. 4,818,192.72

30.____

31. 524,201.52
7,775,678.51
8,345,299.63
40,628,898.08
31,374,670.07

    A. 88,646,647.81   B. 88,646,747.91
    C. 88,648,647.91   D. 88,648,747.81

31.____

32. 6,824,829.40
682,482.94
5,542,015.27
775,678.51
7,732,507.25

    A. 21,557,513.37   B. 21,567,513.37
    C. 22,567,503.37   D. 22,567,513.37

32.____

33. 22,109,405.58
6,097,093.43
5,050,073.99
8,118,050.05
4,313,980.82

    A. 45,688,593.87   B. 45,688,603.87
    C. 45,689,593.87   D. 45,689,603.87

33.____

34. 79,324,114.19
99,848,129.74
43,331,653.31
41,610,207.14

34.____

A. 264,114,104.38
C. 265,114,114.38

B. 264,114,114.38
D. 265,214,104.38

35.   33,729,653.94
     5,959,342.58
   26,052,715.47
    4,452,669.52
    7,079,953.59

35.___

A. 76,374,334.10
C. 77,274,335.10

B. 76,375,334.10
D. 77,275,335.10

Questions 36-40.

DIRECTIONS: Each of Questions 36 through 40 consists of a single number in Column I and four options in Column II. For each question, you are to choose the option (A, B, C, or D) in Column II which *EXACTLY* matches the number in Column I.

SAMPLE QUESTION

Column I	Column II
5965121	A. 5956121
	B. 5965121
	C. 5966121
	D. 5965211

The correct answer is B. Only option B shows the number *EXACTLY* as it appears in Column I. Now answer Questions 36 through 40 in the same manner.

Column I	Column II
36. 9643242	A. 9643242
	B. 9462342
	C. 9642442
	D. 9463242
37. 3572477	A. 3752477
	B. 3725477
	C. 3572477
	D. 3574277
38. 5276101	A. 5267101
	B. 5726011
	C. 5271601
	D. 5276101
39. 4469329	A. 4496329
	B. 4469329
	C. 4496239
	D. 4469239
40. 2326308	A. 2236308
	B. 2233608
	C. 2326308
	D. 2323608

KEY (CORRECT ANSWERS)

1.	D	11.	B	21.	A	31.	D
2.	A	12.	D	22.	C	32.	A
3.	B	13.	A	23.	B	33.	B
4.	D	14.	A	24.	D	34.	A
5.	B	15.	D	25.	A	35.	C
6.	C	16.	D	26.	B	36.	A
7.	A	17.	C	27.	D	37.	C
8.	C	18.	A	28.	A	38.	D
9.	A	19.	D	29.	C	39.	B
10.	B	20.	B	30.	C	40.	C

TEST 2

Questions 1-5.

DIRECTIONS: Each of Questions 1 through 5 consists of a name and a dollar amount. In each question, the name and dollar amount in Column II should be an exact copy of the name and dollar amount in Column I. If there is:

a mistake only in the name, mark your answer A;
a mistake only in the dollar amount, mark your answer B;
a mistake in both the name and the dollar amount, mark your answer C;
no mistake in either the name or the dollar amount, mark your answer D.

SAMPLE QUESTION

Column I	Column II
George Peterson	George Petersson
$125.50	$125.50

Compare the name and dollar amount in Column II with the name and dollar amount in Column I. The name *Petersson* in Column II is spelled *Peterson* in Column I. The amount is the same in both columns. Since there is a mistake only in the name, the answer to the sample question is A.

Now answer Questions 1 through 5 in the same manner.

	Column I	Column II	
1.	Susanne Shultz $3440	Susanne Schultz $3440	1.___
2.	Anibal P. Contrucci $2121.61	Anibel P. Contrucci $2112.61	2.___
3.	Eugenio Mendoza $12.45	Eugenio Mendozza $12.45	3.___
4.	Maurice Gluckstadt $4297	Maurice Gluckstadt $4297	4.___
5.	John Pampellonne $4656.94	John Pammpellonne $4566.94	5.___

Questions 6-11.

DIRECTIONS: Each of Questions 6 through 11 consists of a set of names and addresses which you are to compare. In each question, the name and addresses in Column II should be an *EXACT* copy of the name and address in Column I. If there is:

a mistake only in the name, mark your answer A;
a mistake only in the address, mark your answer B;
a mistake in both the name and address, mark your answer C;
no mistake in either the name or address, mark your answer D.

SAMPLE QUESTION

Column I	Column II
Michael Filbert	Michael Filbert
456 Reade Street	645 Reade Street
New York, N.	New York, N . Y. 10013

Since there is a mistake only in the address (the street number should be 456 instead of 645), the answer to the sample question is B.

Now answer Questions 6 through 11 in the same manner.

Column I	Column II	
6. Hilda Goettelmann 55 Lenox Rd. Brooklyn, N. Y. 11226	Hilda Goettelman 55 Lenox Ave. Brooklyn, N. Y. 11226	6._____
7. Arthur Sherman 2522 Batchelder St. Brooklyn, N. Y. 11235	Arthur Sharman 2522 Batcheder St. Brooklyn, N. Y. 11253	7._____
8. Ralph Barnett 300 West 28 Street New York, New York 10001	Ralph Barnett 300 West 28 Street New York, New York 10001	8._____
9. George Goodwin 135 Palmer Avenue Staten Island, New York 10302	George Godwin 135 Palmer Avenue Staten Island, New York 10302	9._____
10. Alonso Ramirez 232 West 79 Street New York, N. Y. 10024	Alonso Ramirez 223 West 79 Street New York, N. Y. 10024	10._____
11. Cynthia Graham 149-35 83 Street Howard Beach, N. Y. 11414	Cynthia Graham 149-35 83 Street Howard Beach, N. Y. 11414	11._____

Questions 12-20.

DIRECTIONS: Questions 12 through 20 are problems in subtraction. For each question do the subtraction and select your answer from the four choices given.

12. 232,921.85
    -179,587.68   12._____

    A. 52,433.17   B. 52,434.17
    C. 53,334.17   D. 53,343.17

13. 5,531,876.29
    -3,897,158.36   13._____

    A. 1,634,717.93   B. 1,644,718.93
    C. 1,734,717.93   D. 1,734,718.93

14. 1,482,658.22
    - 937,925.76   14._____

    A. 544,633.46   B. 544,732.46
    C. 545,632.46   D. 545,732.46

15. 937,828.17
    -259,673.88   15._____

    A. 678,154.29   B. 679,154.29
    C. 688,155.39   D. 699,155.39

16. 760,412.38
    -263,465.95

    A. 496,046.43   B. 496,946.43
    C. 496,956.43   D. 497,046.43

17. 3,203,902.26
    -2,933,087.96

    A. 260,814.30   B. 269,824.30
    C. 270,814.30   D. 270,824.30

18. 1,023,468.71
    - 934,678.88

    A. 88,780.83   B. 88,789.83
    C. 88,880.83   D. 88,889.83

19. 831,549.47
    -772,814.78

    A. 58,734.69   B. 58,834.69
    C. 59,735,69   D. 59,834.69

20. 6,306,281.74
    -3,617,376.75

    A. 2,687,904.99   B. 2,688,904.99
    C. 2,689,804.99   D. 2,799,905.99

Questions 21-30.

DIRECTIONS: Each of Questions 21 through 30 consists of three lines of code letters and three lines of numbers. The numbers on each line should correspond with the code letters on the same line in accordance with the table below.

Code Letter	J	U	B	T	Y	D	K	R	L	P
Corresponding Number	0	1	2	3	4	5	6	7	8	9

On some of the lines, an error exists in the coding. Compare the letters and numbers in each question carefully. If you find an error or errors on:

only *one* of the lines in the question, mark your answer A;
any *two* lines in the question, mark your answer B;
all *three* lines in the question, mark your answer C;
none of the lines in the question, mark your answer D.

SAMPLE QUESTION

BJRPYUR   2079417
DTBPYKJ   5328460
YKLDBLT   4685283

In the above sample the first line is correct since each code letter listed has the correct corresponding number. On the second line, an error exists because code letter P should have the number 9 instead of the number 8. The third line is correct since each code letter listed has the correct corresponding number. Since there is an error in *one* of the three lines, the correct answer is A.

Now answer Questions 21 through 30 in the same manner.

21.	BYPDTJL	2495308		21.____
	PLRDTJU	9815301		
	DTJRYLK	5207486		
22.	RPBYRJK	7934706		22.____
	PKTYLBU	9624821		
	KDLPJYR	6489047		
23.	TPYBUJR	3942107		23.____
	BYRKPTU	2476931		
	DUKPYDL	5169458		
24.	KBYDLPL	6345898		24.____
	BLRKBRU	2876261		
	JTULDYB	0318542		
25.	LDPYDKR	8594567		25.____
	BDKDRJL	2565708		
	BDRPLUJ	2679810		
26.	PLRLBPU	9858291		26.____
	LPYKRDJ	8936750		
	TDKPDTR	3569527		
27.	RKURPBY	7617924		27.____
	RYUKPTJ	7426930		
	RTKPTJD	7369305		
28.	DYKPBJT	5469203		28.____
	KLPJBTL	6890238		
	TKPLBJP	3698209		
29.	BTPRJYL	2397148		29.____
	LDKUTYR	8561347		
	YDBLRPJ	4528190		
30.	ULPBKYT	1892643		30.____
	KPDTRBJ	6953720		
	YLKJPTB	4860932		

KEY (CORRECT ANSWERS)

1.	A		16.	B
2.	C		17.	C
3.	A		18.	B
4.	D		19.	A
5.	C		20.	B
6.	C		21.	B
7.	C		22.	C
8.	D		23.	D
9.	A		24.	B
10.	B		25.	A
11.	D		26.	C
12.	C		27.	A
13.	A		28.	D
14.	B		29.	B
15.	A		30.	D

CLERICAL ABILITIES

EXAMINATION SECTION
TEST 1

DIRECTIONS: Each question or incomplete statement is followed by several suggested answers or completions. Select the one that BEST answers the question or completes the statement. *PRINT THE LETTER OF THE CORRECT ANSWER IN THE SPACE AT THE RIGHT.*

Questions 1-4.

DIRECTIONS: Questions 1 through 4 are to be answered on the basis of the information given below.

The most commonly used filing system and the one that is easiest to learn is alphabetical filing. This involves putting records in an A to Z order, according to the letters of the alphabet. The name of a person is filed by using the following order: first, the surname or last name; second, the first name; third, the middle name or middle initial. For example, *Henry C. Young* is filed under *Y* and thereafter under *Young, Henry C.* The name of a company is filed in the same way. For example, *Long Cabinet Co.* is filed under *L*, while *John T. Long Cabinet Co.* is filed under *L* and thereafter under *Long., John T. Cabinet Co.*

1. The one of the following which lists the names of persons in the CORRECT alphabetical order is:

    A. Mary Carrie, Helen Carrol, James Carson, John Carter
    B. James Carson, Mary Carrie, John Carter, Helen Carrol
    C. Helen Carrol, James Carson, John Carter, Mary Carrie
    D. John Carter, Helen Carrol, Mary Carrie, James Carson

1.____

2. The one of the following which lists the names of persons in the CORRECT alphabetical order is:

    A. Jones, John C.; Jones, John A.; Jones, John P.; Jones, John K.
    B. Jones, John P.; Jones, John K.; Jones, John C.; Jones, John A.
    C. Jones, John A.; Jones, John C.; Jones, John K.; Jones, John P.
    D. Jones, John K.; Jones, John C.; Jones, John A.; Jones, John P.

2.____

3. The one of the following which lists the names of the companies in the CORRECT alphabetical order is:

    A. Blane Co., Blake Co., Block Co., Blear Co.
    B. Blake Co., Blane Co., Blear Co., Block Co.
    C. Block Co., Blear Co., Blane Co., Blake Co.
    D. Blear Co., Blake Co., Blane Co., Block Co.

3.____

4. You are to return to the file an index card on *Barry C. Wayne Materials and Supplies Co.* Of the following, the CORRECT alphabetical group that you should return the index card to is

    A. A to G   B. H to M   C. N to S   D. T to Z

4.____

Questions 5-10.

DIRECTIONS: In each of Questions 5 through 10, the names of four people are given. For each question, choose as your answer the one of the four names given which should be filed FIRST according to the usual system of alphabetical filing of names, as described in the following paragraph.

In filing names, you must start with the last name. Names are filed in order of the first letter of the last name, then the second letter, etc. Therefore, BAILY would be filed before BROWN, which would be filed before COLT. A name with fewer letters of the same type comes first; i.e., Smith before Smithe. If the last names are the same, the names are filed alphabetically by the first name. If the first name is an initial, a name with an initial would come before a first name that starts with the same letter as the initial. Therefore, I. BROWN would come before IRA BROWN. Finally, if both last name and first name are the same, the name would be filed alphabetically by the middle name, once again an initial coming before a middle name which starts with the same letter as the initial. If there is no middle name at all, the name would come before those with middle initials or names.

Sample Question;   A.   Lester Daniels
                   B.   William Dancer
                   C.   Nathan Danzig
                   D.   Dan Lester

The last names beginning with D are filed before the last name beginning with L. Since DANIELS, DANCER, and DANZIG all begin with the same three letters, you must look at the fourth letter of the last name to determine which name should be filed first. C comes before I or Z in the alphabet, so DANCER is filed before DANIELS or DANZIG. Therefore, the answer to the above sample question is B.

5.   A.   Scott Biala   5._____
     B.   Mary Byala
     C.   Martin Baylor
     D.   Francis Bauer

6.   A.   Howard J. Black   6._____
     B.   Howard Black
     C.   J. Howard Black
     D.   John H. Black

7.   A.   Theodora Garth Kingston   7._____
     B.   Theadore Barth Kingston
     C.   Thomas Kingston
     D.   Thomas T. Kingston

8.   A.   Paulette Mary Huerta   8._____
     B.   Paul M. Huerta
     C.   Paulette L. Huerta
     D.   Peter A. Huerta

9. A. Martha Hunt Morgan   9.____
    B. Martin Hunt Morgan
    C. Mary H. Morgan
    D. Martine H. Morgan

10. A. James T. Meerschaum   10.____
    B. James M. Mershum
    C. James F. Mearshaum
    D. James N. Meshum

Questions 11-14.

DIRECTIONS: Questions 11 through 14 are to be answered SOLELY on the basis of the fol-
              lowing information.

You are required to file various documents in file drawers which are labeled according to
the following pattern:

DOCUMENTS

MEMOS		LETTERS	
File	Subject	File	Subject
84PM1 - (A-L)		84PC1 - (A-L)	
84PM2 - (M-Z)		84PC2 - (M-Z)	

REPORTS		INQUIRIES	
File	Subject	File	Subject
84PR1 - (A-L)		84PQ1 - (A-L)	
84PR2 - (M-Z)		84PQ2 - (M-Z)	

11. A letter dealing with a burglary should be filed in the drawer labeled   11.____

    A. 84PM1   B. 84PC1   C. 84PR1   D. 84PQ2

12. A report on Statistics should be found in the drawer labeled   12.____

    A. 84PM1   B. 84PC2   C. 84PR2   D. 84PQ2

13. An inquiry is received about parade permit procedures. It should be filed in the drawer   13.____
    labeled

    A. 84PM2   B. 84PC1   C. 84PR1   D. 84PQ2

14. A police officer has a question about a robbery report you filed.   14.____
    You should pull this file from the drawer labeled

    A. 84PM1   B. 84PM2   C. 84PR1   D. 84PR2

Questions 15-22.

DIRECTIONS: Each of Questions 15 through 22 consists of four or six numbered names. For
              each question, choose the option (A, B, C, or D) which indicates the order in
              which the names should be filed in accordance with the following filing instruc-
              tions:
    - File alphabetically according to last name, then first name, then middle initial.
    - File according to each successive letter within a name.

- When comparing two names in which, the letters in the longer name are identical to the corresponding letters in the shorter name, the shorter name is filed first.
- When the last names are the same, initials are always filed before names beginning with the same letter.

15.
    I.   Ralph Robinson
    II. Alfred Ross
    III. Luis Robles
    IV. James Roberts
The CORRECT filing sequence for the above names should be

    A. IV, II, I, III   B. I, IV, III, II
    C. III, IV, I, II   D. IV, I, III, II

15.___

16.
    I.   Irwin Goodwin
    II. Inez Gonzalez
    III. Irene Goodman
    IV. Ira S. Goodwin
    V. Ruth I. Goldstein
    VI. M.B. Goodman
The CORRECT filing sequence for the above names should be

    A. V, II, I, IV, III, VI   B. V, II, VI, III, IV, I
    C. V, II, III, VI, IV, I   D. V, II, III, VI, I, IV

16.___

17.
    I.   George Allan
    II. Gregory Allen
    III. Gary Allen
    IV. George Allen
The CORRECT filing sequence for the above names should be

    A. IV, III, I, II   B. I, IV, II, III
    C. III, IV, I, II   D. I, III, IV, II

17.___

18.
    I.   Simon Kauffman
    II. Leo Kaufman
    III. Robert Kaufmann
    IV. Paul Kauffmann
The CORRECT filing sequence for the above names should be

    A. I, IV, II, III   B. II, IV, III, I
    C. III, II, IV, I   D. I, II, III, IV

18.___

19.
    I.   Roberta Williams
    II. Robin Wilson
    III. Roberta Wilson
    IV. Robin Williams
The CORRECT filing sequence for the above names should be

    A. III, II, IV, I   B. I, IV, III, II
    C. I, II, III, IV   D. III, I, II, IV

19.___

20.
    I. Lawrence Shultz   20._____
    II. Albert Schultz
    III. Theodore Schwartz
    IV. Thomas Schwarz
    V. Alvin Schultz
    VI. Leonard Shultz

The CORRECT filing sequence for the above names should be

  A. II, V, III, IV, I, VI   B. IV, III, V, I, II, VI
  C. II, V, I, VI, III, IV   D. I, VI, II, V, III, IV

21.
    I. McArdle   21._____
    II. Mayer
    III. Maletz
    IV. McNiff
    V. Meyer
    VI. MacMahon

The CORRECT filing sequence for the above names should be

  A. I, IV, VI, III, II, V   B. II, I, IV, VI, III, V
  C. VI, III, II, I, IV, V   D. VI, III, II, V, I, IV

22.
    I. Jack E. Johnson   22._____
    II. R.H. Jackson
    III. Bertha Jackson
    IV. J.T. Johnson
    V. Ann Johns
    VI. John Jacobs

The CORRECT filing sequence for the above names should be

  A. II, III, VI, V, IV, I   B. III, II, VI, V, IV, I
  C. VI, II, III, I, V, IV   D. III, II, VI, IV, V, I

Questions 23-30.

DIRECTIONS: The code table below shows 10 letters with matching numbers. For each question, there are three sets of letters. Each set of letters is followed by a set of numbers which may or may not match their correct letter according to the code table. For each question, check all three sets of letters and numbers and mark your answer:
    A. if no pairs are correctly matched
    B. if only one pair is correctly matched
    C. if only two pairs are correctly matched
    D. if all three pairs are correctly matched

CODE TABLE

T	M	V	D	S	P	R	G	B	H
1	2	3	4	5	6	7	8	9	0

Sample Question: TMVDSP - 123456
                       RGBHTM - 789011
                       DSPRGB - 256789

In the sample question above, the first set of numbers correctly matches its set of letters. But the second and third pairs contain mistakes. In the second pair, M is incorrectly matched with number 1. According to the code table, letter M should be correctly matched with number 2. In the third pair, the letter D is incorrectly matched with number 2. According to the code table, letter D should be correctly matched with number 4. Since only one of the pairs is correctly matched, the answer to this sample question is B.

23. RSBMRM 759262   23.____
  GDSRVH 845730
  VDBRTM 349713

24. TGVSDR 183247   24.____
  SMHRDP 520647
  TRMHSR 172057

25. DSPRGM 456782   25.____
  MVDBHT 234902
  HPMDBT 062491

26. BVPTRD 936184   26.____
  GDPHMB 807029
  GMRHMV 827032

27. MGVRSH 283750   27.____
  TRDMBS 174295
  SPRMGV 567283

28. SGBSDM 489542   28.____
  MGHPTM 290612
  MPBMHT 269301

29. TDPBHM 146902   29.____
  VPBMRS 369275
  GDMBHM 842902

30. MVPTBV 236194   30.____
  PDRTMB 647128
  BGTMSM 981232

KEY (CORRECT ANSWERS)

1.	A	11.	B	21.	C
2.	C	12.	C	22.	B
3.	B	13.	D	23.	B
4.	D	14.	D	24.	B
5.	D	15.	D	25.	C
6.	B	16.	C	26.	A
7.	B	17.	D	27.	D
8.	B	18.	A	28.	A
9.	A	19.	B	29.	D
10.	C	20.	A	30.	A

TEST 2

DIRECTIONS: Each question or incomplete statement is followed by several suggested answers or completions. Select the one that BEST answers the question or completes the statement. *PRINT THE LETTER OF THE CORRECT ANSWER IN THE SPACE AT THE RIGHT.*

Questions 1-10.

DIRECTIONS: Questions 1 through 10 each consists of two columns, each containing four lines of names, numbers and/or addresses. For each question, compare the lines in Column I with the lines in Column II to see if they match exactly, and mark your answer A, B, C, or D, according to the following instructions:
- A. all four lines match exactly
- B. only three lines match exactly
- C. only two lines match exactly
- D. only one line matches exactly

		COLUMN I	COLUMN II	
1.	I.	Earl Hodgson	Earl Hodgson	1.___
	II.	1409870	1408970	
	III.	Shore Ave.	Schore Ave.	
	IV.	Macon Rd.	Macon Rd.	
2.	I.	9671485	9671485	2.___
	II.	470 Astor Court	470 Astor Court	
	III.	Halprin, Phillip	Halperin, Phillip	
	IV.	Frank D. Poliseo	Frank D. Poliseo	
3.	I.	Tandem Associates	Tandom Associates	3.___
	II.	144-17 Northern Blvd.	144-17 Northern Blvd.	
	III.	Alberta Forchi	Albert Forchi	
	IV.	Kings Park, NY 10751	Kings Point, NY 10751	
4.	I.	Bertha C. McCormack	Bertha C. McCormack	4.___
	II.	Clayton, MO.	Clayton, MO.	
	III.	976-4242	976-4242	
	IV.	New City, NY 10951	New City, NY 10951	
5.	I.	George C. Morill	George C. Morrill	5.___
	II.	Columbia, SC 29201	Columbia, SD 29201	
	III.	Louis Ingham	Louis Ingham	
	IV.	3406 Forest Ave.	3406 Forest Ave.	
6.	I.	506 S. Elliott Pl.	506 S. Elliott Pl.	6.___
	II.	Herbert Hall	Hurbert Hall	
	III.	4712 Rockaway Pkway	4712 Rockaway Pkway	
	IV.	169 E. 7 St.	169 E. 7 St.	

	COLUMN I	COLUMN II	
7.	I. 345 Park Ave.	345 Park Pl.	7.____
	II. Colman Oven Corp.	Coleman Oven Corp.	
	III. Robert Conte	Robert Conti	
	IV. 6179846	6179846	
8.	I. Grigori Schierber	Grigori Schierber	8.____
	II. Des Moines, Iowa	Des Moines, Iowa	
	III. Gouverneur Hospital	Gouverneur Hospital	
	IV. 91-35 Cresskill Pl.	91-35 Cresskill Pl.	
9.	I. Jeffery Janssen	Jeffrey Janssen	9.____
	II. 8041071	8041071	
	III. 40 Rockefeller Plaza	40 Rockafeller Plaza	
	IV. 407 6 St.	406 7 St.	
10.	I. 5971996	5871996	10.____
	II. 3113 Knickerbocker Ave.	3113 Knickerbocker Ave.	
	III. 8434 Boston Post Rd.	8424 Boston Post Rd.	
	IV. Penn Station	Penn Station	

Questions 11-14.

DIRECTIONS: Questions 11 through 14 are to be answered by looking at the four groups of names and addresses listed below (I, II, III, and IV) and then finding out the number of groups that have their corresponding numbered lines exactly the same.

	GROUP I	GROUP II
Line 1.	Richmond General Hospital	Richman General Hospital
Line 2.	Geriatric Clinic	Geriatric Clinic
Line 3.	3975 Paerdegat St.	3975 Peardegat St.
Line 4	Loudonville, New York 11538	Londonville, New York 11538

	GROUP III	GROUP IV
Line 1.	Richmond General Hospital	Richmend General Hospital
Line 2.	Geriatric Clinic	Geriatric Clinic
Line 3.	3795 Paerdegat St.	3975 Paerdegat St.
Line 4.	Loudonville, New York 11358	Loudonville, New York 11538

11. In how many groups is line one exactly the same?   11.____

    A. Two   B. Three   C. Four   D. None

12. In how many groups is line two exactly the same?   12.____

    A. Two   B. Three   C. Four   D. None

13. In how many groups is line three exactly the same?   13.____

    A. Two   B. Three   C. Four   D. None

14. In how many groups is line four exactly the same?   14.____

    A. Two   B. Three   C. Four   D. None

Questions 15-18.

DIRECTIONS: Each of Questions 15 through 18 has two lists of names and addresses. Each list contains three sets of names and addresses. Check each of the three sets in the list on the right to see if they are the same as the corresponding set in the list on the left. Mark your answers:

    A. if none of the sets in the right list are the same as those in the left list
    B. if only one of the sets in the right list is the same as those in the left list
    C. if only two of the sets in the right list are the same as those in the left list
    D. if all three sets in the right list are the same as those in the left list

15.   Mary T. Berlinger   Mary T. Berlinger   15.____
                2351 Hampton St.   2351 Hampton St.
                Monsey, N.Y. 20117   Monsey, N.Y. 20117

                Eduardo Benes   Eduardo Benes
                473 Kingston Avenue   473 Kingston Avenue
                Central Islip, N.Y. 11734   Central Islip, N.Y. 11734

                Alan Carrington Fuchs   Alan Carrington Fuchs
                17 Gnarled Hollow Road   17 Gnarled Hollow Road
                Los Angeles, CA 91635   Los Angeles, CA 91685

16.   David John Jacobson   David John Jacobson   16.____
                178 35 St. Apt. 4C   178 53 St. Apt. 4C
                New York, N.Y. 00927   New York, N.Y. 00927

                Ann-Marie Calonella   Ann-Marie Calonella
                7243 South Ridge Blvd.   7243 South Ridge Blvd.
                Bakersfield, CA 96714   Bakersfield, CA 96714

                Pauline M. Thompson   Pauline M. Thomson
                872 Linden Ave.   872 Linden Ave.
                Houston, Texas 70321   Houston, Texas 70321

17.   Chester LeRoy Masterton   Chester LeRoy Masterson   17.____
                152 Lacy Rd.   152 Lacy Rd.
                Kankakee, Ill. 54532   Kankakee, Ill. 54532

                William Maloney   William Maloney
                S. LaCrosse Pla.   S. LaCross Pla.
                Wausau, Wisconsin 52146   Wausau, Wisconsin 52146

                Cynthia V. Barnes   Cynthia V. Barnes
                16 Pines Rd.   16 Pines Rd.
                Greenpoint, Miss. 20376   Greenpoint, Miss. 20376

18.   Marcel Jean Frontenac   Marcel Jean Frontenac   18.____
        8 Burton On The Water   6 Burton On The Water
        Calender, Me. 01471   Calender, Me. 01471

        J. Scott Marsden   J. Scott Marsden
        174 S. Tipton St.   174 Tipton St.
        Cleveland, Ohio   Cleveland, Ohio

        Lawrence T. Haney   Lawrence T. Haney
        171 McDonough St.   171 McDonough St.
        Decatur, Ga. 31304   Decatur, Ga. 31304

Questions 19-26.

DIRECTIONS: Each of Questions 19 through 26 has two lists of numbers. Each list contains three sets of numbers. Check each of the three sets in the list on the right to see if they are the same as the corresponding set in the list on the left. Mark your answers:
    A.   if none of the sets in the right list are the same as those in the left list
    B.   if only one of the sets in the right list is the same as those in the left list
    C.   if only two of the sets in the right list are the same as those in the left list
    D.   if all three sets in the right list are the same as those in the left list

19. 7354183476   7354983476   19.____
      4474747744   4474747774
      57914302311   57914302311

20. 7143592185   7143892185   20.____
      8344517699   8344518699
      9178531263   9178531263

21. 2572114731   257214731   21.____
      8806835476   8806835476
      8255831246   8255831246

22. 331476853821   331476858621   22.____
      6976658532996   6976655832996
      3766042113715   3766042113745

23. 8806663315   8806663315   23.____
      74477138449   74477138449
      211756663666   211756663666

24. 990006966996   99000696996   24.____
      53022219743   53022219843
      4171171117717   4171171177717

25. 24400222433004   24400222433004   25.____
      5300030055000355   5300030055500355
      20000075532002022   20000075532002022

26. 6111666406600011116
     71113001170011100733
     26666446664476518

     61116664066001116
     7111300117001100733
     26666446664476518

26.____

Questions 27-30.

DIRECTIONS: Questions 27 through 30 are to be answered by picking the answer which is in the correct numerical order, from the lowest number to the highest number, in each question.

27. A. 44533, 44518, 44516, 44547
     B. 44516, 44518, 44533, 44547
     C. 44547, 44533, 44518, 44516
     D. 44518, 44516, 44547, 44533

27.____

28. A. 95587, 95593, 95601, 95620
     B. 95601, 95620, 95587, 95593
     C. 95593, 95587, 95601, 95620
     D. 95620, 95601, 95593, 95587

28.____

29. A. 232212, 232208, 232232, 232223
     B. 232208, 232223, 232212, 232232
     C. 232208, 232212, 232223, 232232
     D. 232223, 232232, 232208, 232212

29.____

30. A. 113419, 113521, 113462, 113588
     B. 113588, 113462, 113521, 113419
     C. 113521, 113588, 113419, 113462
     D. 113419, 113462, 113521, 113588

30.____

KEY (CORRECT ANSWERS)

1.	C	11.	A	21.	C
2.	B	12.	C	22.	A
3.	D	13.	A	23.	D
4.	A	14.	A	24.	A
5.	C	15.	C	25.	C
6.	B	16.	B	26.	C
7.	D	17.	B	27.	B
8.	A	18.	B	28.	A
9.	D	19.	B	29.	C
10.	C	20.	B	30.	D

RECORD KEEPING
EXAMINATION SECTION
TEST 1

DIRECTIONS: Each question or incomplete statement is followed by several suggested answers or completions. Select the one that BEST answers the question or completes the statement. *PRINT THE LETTER OF THE CORRECT ANSWER IN THE SPACE AT THE RIGHT.*

Questions 1-7.

DIRECTIONS: In answering Questions 1 through 7, use the following master list. For each question, determine where the name would fit on the master list. Each answer choice indicates right before or after the name in the answer choice.

Aaron, Jane
Armstead, Brendan
Bailey, Charles
Dent, Ricardo
Grant, Mark
Mars, Justin
Methieu, Justine
Parker, Cathy
Sampson, Suzy
Thomas, Heather

1. Schmidt, William
A. Right before Cathy Parker
B. Right after Heather Thomas
C. Right after Suzy Sampson
D. Right before Ricardo Dent

1.____

2. Asanti, Kendall
A. Right before Jane Aaron
B. Right after Charles Bailey
C. Right before Justine Methieu
D. Right after Brendan Armstead

2.____

3. O'Brien, Daniel
A. Right after Justine Methieu
B. Right before Jane Aaron
C. Right after Mark Grant
D. Right before Suzy Sampson

3.____

4. Marrow, Alison
A. Right before Cathy Parker
B. Right before Justin Mars
C. Right after Mark Grant
D. Right after Heather Thomas

4.____

5. Grantt, Marissa
A. Right before Mark Grant
B. Right after Mark Grant
C. Right after Justin Mars
D. Right before Suzy Sampson

5.____

6. Thompson, Heath   6.____
    A. Right after Justin Mars   B. Right before Suzy Sampson
    C. Right after Heather Thomas   D. Right before Cathy Parker

DIRECTIONS: Before answering Question 7, add in all of the names from Questions 1 through
              6. Then fit the name in alphabetical order based on the new list.

7. Francisco, Mildred   7.____
    A. Right before Mark Grant   B. Right after Marissa Grantt
    C. Right before Alison Marrow   D. Right after Kendall Asanti

Questions 8-10.

DIRECTIONS: In answering Questions 8 through 10, compare each pair of names and
              addresses. Indicate whether they are the same or different in any way.

8. William H. Pratt, J.D.   William H. Pratt, J.D.   8.____
    Attourney at Law   Attorney at Law
    A. No differences   B. 1 difference
    C. 2 differences   D. 3 differences

9. 1303 Theater Drive,; Apt. 3-B   1330 Theatre Drive,; Apt. 3-B   9.____
    A. No differences   B. 1 difference
    C. 2 differences   D. 3 differences

10. Petersdorff, Briana and Mary   Petersdorff, Briana and Mary   10.____
    A. No differences   B. 1 difference
    C. 2 differences   D. 3 differences

11. Which of the following words, if any, are misspelled?   11.____
    A. Affordable   B. Circumstansial
    C. Legalese   D. None of the above

Questions 12-13.

DIRECTIONS: Questions 12 and 13 are to be answered on the basis of the following table.

Standardized Test Results for High School Students in District #1230

	English	Math	Science	Reading
High School 1	21	22	15	18
High School 2	12	16	13	15
High School 3	16	18	21	17
High School 4	19	14	15	16

The scores for each high school in the district were averaged out and listed for each
subject tested. Scores of 0-10 are significantly below College Readiness Standards. 11-15 are
below College Readiness, 16-20 meet College Readiness, and 21-25 are above College
Readiness.

12. If the high schools need to meet or exceed in at least half the categories
in order to NOT be considered "at risk," which schools are considered "at risk"?
   A. High School 2   B. High School 3
   C. High School 4   D. Both A and C

12.____

13. What percentage of subjects did the district as a whole meet or exceed
College Readiness standards?
   A. 25%   B. 50%   C. 75%   D. 100%

13.____

Questions 14-15.

DIRECTIONS: Questions 14 and 15 are to be answered on the basis of the following
information.

You have seven employees working as a part of your team: Austin, Emily, Jeremy,
Christina, Martin, Harriet, and Steve. You have just sent an e-mail informing them that
there will be a mandatory training session next week. To ensure that work still gets done,
you are offering the training twice during the week: once on Tuesday and also on
Thursday. This way half the employees will still be working while the other half attend the
training. The only other issue is that Jeremy doesn't work on Tuesdays and Harriet
doesn't work on Thursdays due to compressed work schedules.

14. Which of the following is a possible attendance roster for the first training
session?
   A. Emily, Jeremy, Steve   B. Steve, Christina, Harriet
   C. Harriet, Jeremy, Austin   D. Steve, Martin, Jeremy

14.____

15. If Harriet, Christina, and Steve attend the training session on Tuesday, which
of the following is a possible roster for Thursday's training session?
   A. Jeremy, Emily, and Austin   B. Emily, Martin, and Harriet
   C. Austin, Christina, and Emily   D. Jeremy, Emily, and Steve

15.____

Questions 16-20.

DIRECTIONS: In answering Questions 16 through 20, you will be given a word and will need
to choose the answer choice that is MOST similar or different to the word.

16. Which word means the SAME as *annual*?
   A. Monthly   B. Usually   C. Yearly   D. Constantly

16.____

17. Which word means the SAME as *effort*?
   A. Energy   B. Equate   C. Cherish   D. Commence

17.____

18. Which word means the OPPOSITE of *forlorn*?
   A. Neglected   B. Lethargy   C. Optimistic   D. Astonished

18.____

19. Which word means the SAME as *risk*?
   A. Admire   B. Hazard   C. Limit   D. Hesitant

19.____

20. Which word means the OPPOSITE of *translucent*?　　　　　　　　20.____
    A. Opaque　　　　　B. Transparent　C. Luminous　　D. Introverted

21. Last year, Jamie's annual salary was $50,000. Her boss called her today　21.____
    to inform her that she would receive a 20% raise for the upcoming year. How
    much more money will Jamie receive next year?
    A. $60,000　　　　B. $10,000　　　C. $1,000　　　D. $51,000

22. You and a co-worker work for a temp hiring agency as part of their office　22.____
    staff. You both are given 6 days off per month. How many days off are you
    and your co-worker given in a year?
    A. 24　　　　　　B. 72　　　　　C. 144　　　　D. 48

23. If Margot makes $34,000 per year and she works 40 hours per week for　23.____
    all 52 weeks, what is her hourly rate?
    A. $16.34/hour　　B. $17.00/hour　C. $15.54/hour　D. $13.23/hour

24. How many dimes are there in $175.00?　　　　　　　　　　24.____
    A. 175　　　　　　B. 1,750　　　　C. 3,500　　　D. 17,500

25. If Janey is three times as old as Emily, and Emily is 3, how old is Janey?　25.____
    A. 6　　　　　　　B. 9　　　　　C. 12　　　　D. 15

KEY (CORRECT ANSWERS)

1.	C		11.	B
2.	D		12.	A
3.	A		13.	D
4.	B		14.	B
5.	B		15.	A
6.	C		16.	C
7.	A		17.	A
8.	B		18.	C
9.	C		19.	B
10.	A		20.	A

21.	B
22.	C
23.	A
24.	B
25.	B

TEST 2

DIRECTIONS: Each question or incomplete statement is followed by several suggested answers or completions. Select the one that BEST answers the question or completes the statement. *PRINT THE LETTER OF THE CORRECT ANSWER IN THE SPACE AT THE RIGHT.*

Questions 1-6.

DIRECTIONS: Questions 1 through 6 are to be answered on the basis of the following information.

item	name of item to be ordered
quantity	minimum number that can be ordered
beginning amount	amount in stock at start of month
amount received	amount receiving during month
ending amount	amount in stock at end of month
amount used	amount used during month
amount to order	will need at least as much of each item as used in the previous month
unit price	cost of each unit of an item
total price	total price for the order

Item	Quantity	Beginning	Received	Ending	Amount Used	Amount to Order	Unit Price	Total Price
Pens	10	22	10	8	24	20	$0.11	$2.20
Spiral notebooks	8	30	13	12			$0.25	
Binder clips	2 boxes	3 boxes	1 box	1 box			$1.79	
Sticky notes	3 packs	12 packs	4 packs	2 packs			$1.29	
Dry erase markers	1 pack (dozen)	34 markers	8 markers	40 markers			$16.49	
Ink cartridges (printer)	1 cartridge	3 cartridges	1 cartridge	2 cartridges			$79.99	
Folders	10 folders	25 folders	15 folders	10 folders			$1.08	

1. How many packs of sticky notes were used during the month?   1.____
   A. 16   B. 10   C. 12   D. 14

2. How many folders need to be ordered for next month?   2.____
   A. 15   B. 20   C. 30   D. 40

3. What is the total price of notebooks that you will need to order?   3.____
   A. $6.00   B. $0.25   C. $4.50   D. $2.75

4. Which of the following will you spend the second most money on?   4.____
   A. Ink cartridges   B. Dry erase markers
   C. Sticky notes   D. Binder clips

5. How many packs of dry erase markers should you order?   5.____
   A. 1   B. 8   C. 12   D. 0

6. What will be the total price of the file folders you order?   6._____
    A. $20.16   B. $2.16   C. $1.08   D. $4.32

Questions 7-11.

DIRECTIONS: Questions 7 through 11 are to be answered on the basis of the following table.

Number of Car Accidents, By Location and Cause, for 2014						
	Location 1		Location 2		Location 3	
Cause	Number	Percent	Number	Percent	Number	Percent
Severe Weather	10		25		30	
Excessive Speeding	20	40	5		10	
Impaired Driving	15		15	25	8	
Miscellaneous	5		15		2	4
TOTALS	50	100	60	100	50	100

7. Which of the following is the third highest cause of accidents for all three   7._____
locations?
    A. Severe Weather   B. Impaired Driving
    C. Miscellaneous   D. Excessive Speeding

8. The average number of Severe Weather accidents per week at Location 3   8._____
for the year (52 weeks) was MOST NEARLY
    A. 0.57   B. 30   C. 1   D. 1.25

9. Which location had the LARGEST percentage of accidents caused by   9._____
Impaired Driving?
    A. 1   B. 2   C. 3   D. Both A and B

10. If one-third of the accidents at all three locations resulted in at least one   10._____
fatality, what is the LEAST amount of deaths caused by accidents last year?
    A. 60   B. 106   C. 66   D. 53

11. What is the percentage of accidents caused by miscellaneous means from   11._____
all three locations in 2014?
    A. 5%   B. 10%   C. 13%   D. 25%

12. How many pairs of the following groups of letters are exactly alike?   12._____
    ACDOBJ   ACDBOJ
    HEWBWR   HEWRWB
    DEERVS   DEERVS
    BRFQSX   BRFQSX
    WEYRVB   WEYRVB
    SPQRZA   SQRPZA

    A. 2   B. 3   C. 4   D. 5

Questions 13-19.

DIRECTIONS: Questions 13 through 19 are to be answered on the basis of the following
              information.

In 2012, the most current information on the American population was finished. The
information was compiled by 200 volunteers in each of the 50 states. The territory of Puerto
Rico, a sovereign of the United States, had 25 people assigned to compile data. In February of
2010, volunteers in each state and sovereign began collecting information. In Puerto Rico, data
collection finished by January 31st, 2011, while work in the United States was completed on
June 30, 2012. Each volunteer gathered data on the population of their state or sovereign.
When the information was compiled, volunteers sent reports to the nation's capital, Washington,
D.C. Each volunteer worked 20 hours per month and put together 10 reports per month. After
the data was compiled in total, 50 people reviewed the data and worked from January 2012 to
December 2012.

13. How many reports were generated from February 2010 to April 2010 in Illinois   13._____
     and Ohio?
        A. 3,000   B. 6,000   C. 12,000   D. 15,000

14. How many volunteers in total collected population data in January 2012?   14._____
        A. 10,000   B. 2,000   C. 225   D. 200

15. How many reports were put together in May 2012?   15._____
        A. 2,000   B. 50,000   C. 100,000   D. 100,250

16. How many hours did the Puerto Rican volunteers work in the fall   16._____
     (September-November)?
        A. 60   B. 500   C. 1,500   D. 0

17. How many workers were compiling or reviewing data in July 2012?   17._____
        A. 25   B. 50   C. 200   D. 250

18. What was the total amount of hours worked by Nevada volunteers in July 2010?   18._____
        A. 500   B. 4,000   C. 4,500   D. 5,000

19. How many reviewers worked in January 2013?   19._____
        A. 75   B. 50   C. 0   D. 25

20. John has to file 10 documents per shelf. How many documents would it   20._____
     take for John to fill 40 shelves?
        A. 40   B. 400   C. 4,500   D. 5,000

21. Jill wants to travel from New York City to Los Angeles by bike, which   21._____
     is approximately 2,772 miles. How many miles per day would Jill need to
     average if she wanted to complete the trip in 4 weeks?
        A. 100   B. 89   C. 99   D. 94

22. If there are 24 CPU's and only 7 monitors, how many more monitors do
you need to have the same amount of monitors as CPU's?
   A. Not enough information   B. 17
   C. 31   D. 0

22._____

23. If Gerry works 5 days a week and 8 hours each day, and John works 3 days
a week and 10 hours each day, how many more hours per year will Gerry work
than John?
   A. They work the same amount of hours.
   B. 450
   C. 520
   D. 832

23._____

24. Jimmy gets transferred to a new office. The new office has 25 employees,
but only 16 are there due to a blizzard. How many coworkers was Jimmy able
to meet on his first day?
   A. 16   B. 25   C. 9   D. 7

24._____

25. If you do a fundraiser for charities in your area and raise $500 total, how
much would you give to each charity if you were donating equal amounts to 3
of them?
   A. $250.00   B. $167.77   C. $50.00   D. $111.11

25._____

KEY (CORRECT ANSWERS)

1.	D		11.	C
2.	B		12.	B
3.	A		13.	C
4.	C		14.	A
5.	D		15.	C
6.	B		16.	C
7.	D		17.	B
8.	A		18.	B
9.	A		19.	C
10.	D		20.	B

21.	C
22.	B
23.	C
24.	A
25.	B

TEST 3

DIRECTIONS: Each question or incomplete statement is followed by several suggested answers or completions. Select the one that BEST answers the question or completes the statement. *PRINT THE LETTER OF THE CORRECT ANSWER IN THE SPACE AT THE RIGHT.*

Questions 1-3.

DIRECTIONS: In answering Questions 1 through 3, choose the correctly spelled word.

1. A. allusion   B. alusion   C. allusien   D. allution   1.____

2. A. altitude   B. alltitude   C. atlitude   D. altlitude   2.____

3. A. althogh   B. allthough   C. althrough   D. although   3.____

Questions 4-9.

DIRECTIONS: In answering Questions 4 through 9, choose the answer that BEST completes the analogy.

4. Odometer is to mileage as compass is to   4.____
   A. speed   B. needle   C. hiking   D. direction

5. Marathon is to race as hibernation is to   5.____
   A. winter   B. dream   C. sleep   D. bear

6. Cup is to coffee as bowl is to   6.____
   A. dish   B. spoon   C. food   D. soup

7. Flow is to river as stagnant is to   7.____
   A. pool   B. rain   C. stream   D. canal

8. Paw is to cat as hoof is to   8.____
   A. lamb   B. horse   C. lion   D. elephant

9. Architect is to building as sculptor is to   9.____
   A. museum   B. chisel   C. stone   D. statue

Questions 10-14.

DIRECTIONS: Questions 10 through 14 are to be answered on the basis of the following graph.

Population of Carroll City Broken Down by Age and Gender (in Thousands)			
Age	Female	Male	Total
Under 15	60	60	120
15-23		22	
24-33		20	44
34-43	13	18	31
44-53	20		67
64 and Over	65	65	130
TOTAL	230	232	462

10.   How many people in the city are between the ages of 15-23?   10.____
   A. 70   B. 46,000   C. 70,000   D. 225,000

11.   Approximately what percentage of the total population of the city was   11.____
   female aged 24-33?
   A. 10%   B. 5%   C. 15%   D. 25%

12.   If 33% of the males have a job and 55% of females don't have a job,   12.____
   which of the following statements is TRUE?
   A. Males have approximately 2,600 more jobs than females.
   B. Females have approximately 49,000 more jobs than males.
   C. Females have approximately 26,000 more jobs than males.
   D. None of the above statements are true.

13.   How many females between the ages of 15-23 live in Carroll City?   13.____
   A. 67,000   B. 24,000   C. 48,000   D. 91,000

14.   Assume all males 44-53 living in Carroll City are employed. If two-thirds   14.____
   of males age 44-53 work jobs outside of Carroll City, how many work within city limits?
   A. 31,333
   B. 15,667
   C. 47,000
   D. Cannot answer the question with the information provided

Questions 15-16.

DIRECTIONS: Questions 15 and 16 are labeled as shown. Alphabetize them for filing.
Choose the answer that correctly shows the order.

15.   (1)   AED   15.____
(2)   OOS
(3)   FOA
(4)   DOM
(5)   COB

A. 2-5-4-3-2   B. 1-4-5-2-3   C. 1-5-4-2-3   D. 1-5-4-3-2

16.   Alphabetize the names of the people. Last names are given last.   16.____
(1)   Lindsey Jamestown
(2)   Jane Alberta
(3)   Ally Jamestown
(4)   Allison Johnston
(5)   Lyle Moreno

A. 2-1-3-4-5   B. 3-4-2-1-5   C. 2-3-1-4-5   D. 4-3-2-1-5

17.   Which of the following words is misspelled?   17.____
A. disgust   B. whisper
C. locale   D. none of the above

Questions 18-21.

DIRECTIONS: Questions 18 through 21 are to be answered on the basis of the following list of
employees.

Robertson, Aaron
Bacon, Gina
Jerimiah, Trace
Gillette, Stanley
Jacks, Sharon

18.   Which employee name would come in third in alphabetized list?   18.____
A. Robertson, Aaron   B. Jerimiah, Trace
C. Gillette, Stanley   D. Jacks, Sharon

19.   Which employee's first name starts with the letter in the alphabet that is   19.____
five letters after the first letter of their last name?
A. Jerimiah, Trace   B. Bacon, Gina
C. Jacks, Sharon   D. Gillette, Stanley

20.   How many employees have last names that are exactly five letters long?   20.____
A. 1   B. 2   C. 3   D. 4

21. How many of the employees have either a first or last name that starts with the letter "G"?
   A. 1
   B. 2
   C. 4
   D. 5

21.____

Questions 22-25.

DIRECTIONS: Questions 22 through 25 are to be answered on the basis of the following chart.

Bicycle Sales (Model #34JA32)							
Country	May	June	July	August	September	October	Total
Germany	34	47	45	54	56	60	296
Britain	40	44	36	47	47	46	260
Ireland	37	32	32	32	34	33	200
Portugal	14	14	14	16	17	14	89
Italy	29	29	28	31	29	31	177
Belgium	22	24	24	26	25	23	144
Total	176	198	179	206	208	207	1166

22. What percentage of the overall total was sold to the German importer?
   A. 25.3%
   B. 22%
   C. 24.1%
   D. 23%

22.____

23. What percentage of the overall total was sold in September?
   A. 24.1%
   B. 25.6%
   C. 17.9%
   D. 24.6%

23.____

24. What is the average number of units per month imported into Belgium over the first four months shown?
   A. 26
   B. 20
   C. 24
   D. 31

24.____

25. If you look at the three smallest importers, what is their total import percentage?
   A. 35.1%
   B. 37.1%
   C. 40%
   D. 28%

25.____

KEY (CORRECT ANSWERS)

1.	A		11.	B
2.	A		12.	C
3.	D		13.	C
4.	D		14.	B
5.	C		15.	D
6.	D		16.	C
7.	A		17.	D
8.	B		18.	D
9.	D		19.	B
10.	C		20.	B

21.	B
22.	A
23.	C
24.	C
25.	A

TEST 4

DIRECTIONS: Each question or incomplete statement is followed by several suggested answers or completions. Select the one that BEST answers the question or completes the statement. *PRINT THE LETTER OF THE CORRECT ANSWER IN THE SPACE AT THE RIGHT.*

Questions 1-6.

DIRECTIONS: In answering Questions 1 through 6, choose the sentence that represents the BEST example of English grammar.

1. A. Joey and me want to go on a vacation next week.   1.____
   B. Gary told Jim he would need to take some time off.
   C. If turning six years old, Jim's uncle would teach Spanish to him.
   D. Fax a copy of your resume to Ms. Perez and me.

2. A. Jerry stood in line for almost two hours.   2.____
   B. The reaction to my engagement was less exciting than I thought it would be.
   C. Carlos and me have done great work on this project.
   D. Two parts of the speech needs to be revised before tomorrow.

3. A. Arriving home, the alarm was tripped.   3.____
   B. Jonny is regarded as a stand up guy, a responsible parent, and he doesn't give up until a task is finished.
   C. Each employee must submit a drug test each month.
   D. One of the documents was incinerated in the explosion.

4. A. As soon as my parents get home, I told them I finished all of my chores.   4.____
   B. I asked my teacher to send me my missing work, check my absences, and how did I do on my test.
   C. Matt attempted to keep it concealed from Jenny and me.
   D. If Mary or him cannot get work done on time, I will have to split them up.

5. A. Driving to work, the traffic report warned him of an accident on Highway 47.   5.____
   B. Jimmy has performed well this season.
   C. Since finishing her degree, several job offers have been given to Cam.
   D. Our boss is creating unstable conditions for we employees.

6. A. The thief was described as a tall man with a wiry mustache weighing approximately 150 pounds.   6.____
   B. She gave Patrick and I some more time to finish our work.
   C. One of the books that he ordered was damaged in shipping.
   D. While talking on the rotary phone, the car Jim was driving skidded off the road.

Questions 7-9.

DIRECTIONS: Questions 7 through 9 are to be answered on the basis of the following graph.

Ice Lake Frozen Flight (2002-2013)		
Year	Number of Participants	Temperature (Fahrenheit)
2002	22	4°
2003	50	33°
2004	69	18°
2005	104	22°
2006	108	24°
2007	288	33°
2008	173	9°
2009	598	39°
2010	698	26°
2011	696	30°
2012	777	28°
2013	578	32°

7. Which two year span had the LARGEST difference between temperatures?   7.____
   A. 2002 and 2003   B. 2011 and 2012
   C. 2008 and 2009   D. 2003 and 2004

8. How many total people participated in the years after the temperature   8.____
   reached at least 29°?
   A. 2,295   B. 1,717   C. 2,210   D. 4,543

9. In 2007, the event saw 288 participants, while in 2008 that number   9.____
   dropped to 173. Which of the following reasons BEST explains the drop in
   participants?
   A. The event had not been going on that long and people didn't know about
      it.
   B. The lake water wasn't cold enough to have people jump in.
   C. The temperature was too cold for many people who would have normally
      participated.
   D. None of the above reasons explain the drop in participants.

10. In the following list of numbers, how many times does 4 come just after 2   10.____
    when 2 comes just after an odd number?
    23652476538986324885724863924 24
    A. 2   B. 3   C. 4   D. 5

11. Which choice below lists the letter that is as far after B as S is after N in   11.____
    the alphabet?
    A. G   B. H   C. I   D. J

Questions 12-15.

DIRECTIONS: Questions 12 through 15 are to be answered on the basis of the following
              directory and list of changes.

Directory		
Name	Emp. Type	Position
Julie Taylor	Warehouse	Packer
James King	Office	Administrative Assistant
John Williams	Office	Salesperson
Ray Moore	Warehouse	Maintenance
Kathleen Byrne	Warehouse	Supervisor
Amy Jones	Office	Salesperson
Paul Jonas	Office	Salesperson
Lisa Wong	Warehouse	Loader
Eugene Lee	Office	Accountant
Bruce Lavine	Office	Manager
Adam Gates	Warehouse	Packer
Will Suter	Warehouse	Packer
Gary Lorper	Office	Accountant
Jon Adams	Office	Salesperson
Susannah Harper	Office	Salesperson

Directory Updates:
- Employee e-mail address will adhere to the following guidelines:
  lastnamefirstname@apexindustries.com (ex. Susannah Harper is
  harpersusannah@apexindustries.com). Currently, employees in the warehouse
  share one e-mail, distribution@apexindustries.com.
- The "Loader" position was now be referred to as "Specialist I"
- Adam Gates has accepted a Supervisor position within the Warehouse and is no
  longer a Packer. All warehouses employees report to the two Supervisors and all
  office employees report to the Manager.

12. Amy Jones tried to send an e-mail to Adam Gates, but it wouldn't send.   12._____
    Which of the following offers the BEST explanation?
    A. Amy put Adam's first name first and then his last name.
    B. Adam doesn't check his e-mail, so he wouldn't know if he received the e-
       mail or not.
    C. Adam does not have his own e-mail.
    D. Office employees are not allowed to send e-mails to each other.

13. How many Packers currently work for Apex Industries?   13._____
    A. 2   B. 3   C. 4   D. 5

14. What position does Lisa Wong currently hold?   14._____
    A. Specialist I   B. Secretary
    C. Administrative Assistant   D. Loader

15. If an employee wanted to contact the office manager, which of the
    following e-mails should the e-mail be sent to?
    A. officemanager@apexindustries.com
    B. brucelavine@apexindustries.com
    C. lavinebruce@apexindustries.com
    D. distribution@apexindustries.com

15.____

Questions 16-19.

DIRECTIONS: In answering Questions 16 through 19, compare the three names, numbers or
addresses.

16. Smiley Yarnell   Smiley Yarnel   Smily Yarnell   16.____
    A. All three are exactly alike.
    B. The first and second are exactly alike.
    C. The second and third are exactly alike.
    D. All three are different.

17. 1583 Theater Drive   1583 Theater Drive   1583 Theatre Drive   17.____
    A. All three are exactly alike.
    B. The first and second are exactly alike.
    C. The second and third are exactly alike.
    D. All three are different.

18. 3341893212   3341893212   3341893212   18.____
    A. All three are exactly alike.
    B. The first and second are exactly alike.
    C. The second and third are exactly alike.
    D. All three are different.

19. Douglass Watkins   Douglas Watkins   Douglass Watkins   19.____
    A. All three are exactly alike.
    B. The first and third are exactly alike.
    C. The second and third are exactly alike.
    D. All three are different.

Questions 20-24.

DIRECTIONS: In answering Questions 20 through 24, you will be presented with a word.
Choose the synonym that BEST represents the word in question.

20. Flexible   20.____
    A. delicate   B. inflammable   C. strong   D. pliable

21. Alternative   21.____
    A. choice   B. moderate   C. lazy   D. value

22. Corroborate
    A. examine   B. explain   C. verify   D. explain   22.____

23. Respiration
    A. recovery   B. breathing   C. sweating   D. selfish   23.____

24. Negligent
    A. lazy   B. moderate   C. hopeless   D. lax   24.____

25. Plumber is to Wrench as Painter is to   25.____
    A. pipe   B. shop   C. hammer   D. brush

KEY (CORRECT ANSWERS)

1.	D		11.	A
2.	A		12.	C
3.	D		13.	A
4.	C		14.	A
5.	B		15.	C
6.	C		16.	D
7.	C		17.	B
8.	B		18.	A
9.	C		19.	B
10.	C		20.	D

21.	A
22.	C
23.	B
24.	D
25.	D

NAME and NUMBER COMPARISONS

COMMENTARY

This test seeks to measure your ability and disposition to do a job carefully and accurately, your attention to exactness and preciseness of detail, your alertness and versatility in discerning similarities and differences between things, and your power in systematically handling written language symbols.

It is actually a test of your ability to do academic and/or clerical work, using the basic elements of verbal (qualitative) and mathematical (quantitative) learning – words <u>and</u> numbers.

EXAMINATION SECTION
TEST 1

Tests 1-2

DIRECTIONS: Questions 1 through 6 consist of sets of names and addresses. In each question, the name and address in Column II should be an exact copy of the name and address in Column I. *PRINT IN THE SPACE AT THE RIGHT THE LETTER:*
- A. if there is a mistake only in the name
- B. if there is a mistake only in the address
- C. if there is a mistake in both name and address
- D. if there is no mistake in either name or address

SAMPLE:

Michael Filbert	Michael Filbert
456 Reade Street	645 Reade Street
New York, N.Y. 10013	New York, N.Y. 10013

Since there is a mistake only in the address, the answer is B.

1.	Esta Wong 141 West 68 St. New York, N.Y. 10023	Esta Wang 141 West 68 St. New York, N.Y. 10023	1.____
2.	Dr. Alberto Grosso 3475 12th Avenue Brooklyn, N.Y. 11218	Dr. Alberto Grosso 3475 12th Avenue Brooklyn, N.Y. 11218	2.____
3.	Mrs. Ruth Bortlas 482 Theresa Ct. Far Rockaway, N.Y. 11691	Ms. Ruth Bortlas 482 Theresa Ct. Far Rockaway, N.Y. 11169	3.____
4.	Mr. and Mrs. Howard Fox 2301 Sedgwick Ave. Bronx, N.Y. 10468	Mr. and Mrs. Howard Fox 231 Sedgwick Ave. Bronx, N.Y. 10468	4.____
5.	Miss Marjorie Black 223 East 23 Street New York, N.Y. 10010	Miss Margorie Black 223 East 23 Street New York, N.Y. 10010	5.____

6. Michelle Herman
   806 Valley Rd.
   Old Tappan, N.J. 07675

   Michelle Hermann
   806 Valley Dr.
   Old Tappan, N.J. 07675

6. ____

————

KEY (CORRECT ANSWERS)

1. A
2. D
3. C
4. B
5. A
6. C

————

TEST 2

DIRECTIONS: Questions 1 through 6 consist of sets of names and addresses. In each question, the name and address in Column II should be an exact copy of the name and address in Column I. *PRINT IN THE SPACE AT THE RIGHT THE LETTER:*

    A. if there is a mistake only in the name
    B. if there is a mistake only in the address
    C. if there is a mistake in both name and address
    D. if there is no mistake in either name or address

1. Ms. Joan Kelly
    313 Franklin Ave.
    Brooklyn, N.Y. 11202

    Ms. Joan Kielly
    318 Franklin Ave.
    Brooklyn, N.Y. 11202
    1._____

2. Mrs. Eileen Engel
    47-24 86 Road
    Queens, N.Y. 11122

    Mrs. Ellen Engel
    47-24 86 Road
    Queens, N.Y. 11122
    2._____

3. Marcia Michaels
    213 E. 81 St.
    New York, N.Y. 10012

    Marcia Michaels
    213 E. 81 St.
    New York, N.Y. 10012
    3._____

4. Rev. Edward J. Smyth
    1401 Brandeis Street
    San Francisco, Calif. 96201

    Rev. Edward J. Smyth
    1401 Brandies Street
    San Francisco, Calif. 96201
    4._____

5. Alicia Rodriguez
    24-68 81 St.
    Elmhurst, N.Y. 11122

    Alicia Rodriquez
    2468 81 St.
    Elmhurst, N.Y. 11122
    5._____

6. Ernest Eisemann
    21 Columbia St.
    New York, N.Y. 10007

    Ernest Eisermann
    21 Columbia St.
    New York, N.Y. 10007
    6._____

KEY (CORRECT ANSWERS)

    1. C
    2. A
    3. D
    4. B
    5. C
    6. A

TEST 3

DIRECTIONS: Questions 1 through 8 consist of names, locations and telephone numbers. In each question, the name, location and number in Column II should be an exact copy of the name, location and number in Column I. *PRINT IN THE SPACE AT THE RIGHT THE LETTER:*

A. if there is a mistake in one line only
B. if there is a mistake in two lines only
C. if there is a mistake in three lines only
D. if there are no mistakes in any of the lines

1. Ruth Lang   Ruth Lang   1.___
   EAM Bldg., Room C101   EAM Bldg., Room C110
   625-2000, ext. 765   625-2000, ext. 765

2. Anne Marie Ionozzi   Anna Marie Ionozzi   2.___
   Investigations, Room 827   Investigation, Room 827
   576-4000, ext. 832   566-4000, ext. 832

3. Willard Jameson   Willard Jamieson   3.___
   Fm C Bldg. Room 687   Fm C Bldg. Room 687
   454-3010   454-3010

4. Joanne Zimmermann   Joanne Zimmermann   4.___
   Bldg. SW, Room 314   Bldg. SW, Room 314
   532-4601   532-4601

5. Carlyle Whetstone   Caryle Whetstone   5.___
   Payroll Division-A, Room 212A   Payroll Division-A, Room 212A
   262-5000, ext. 471   262-5000, ext. 417

6. Kenneth Chiang   Kenneth Chiang   6.___
   Legal Council, Room 9745   Legal Counsel, Room 9745
   (201) 416-9100, ext. 17   (201) 416-9100, ext. 17

7. Ethel Koenig   Ethel Hoenig   7.___
   Personnel Services Div, Rm 433   Personal Services Div, Rm 433
   635-7572   635-7527

8. Joyce Ehrhardt   Joyce Ehrhart   8.___
   Office of Administrator, Rm W56   Office of Administrator, Rm W56
   387-8706   387-7806

KEY (CORRECT ANSWERS)

1. A
2. C
3. A
4. D
5. B

6. A
7. C
8. B

———

TEST 4

DIRECTIONS: Each of questions 1 through 10 gives the identification number and name of a person who has received treatment at a certain hospital. You are to choose the option (A, B, C or D) which has EXACTLY the same number and name as those given in the question.

SAMPLE:
123765 Frank Y. Jones
- A. 123675 Frank Y. Jones
- B. 123765 Frank T. Jones
- C. 123765 Frank Y. Johns
- D. 123765 Frank Y. Jones

The correct answer is D, because it is the only option showing the identification number and name exactly as they are in the sample question.

1. 754898 Diane Malloy   1.___

- A. 745898 Diane Malloy
- B. 754898 Dion Malloy
- C. 754898 Diane Malloy
- D. 754898 Diane Maloy

2. 661818 Ferdinand Figueroa   2.___

- A. 661818 Ferdinand Figeuroa
- B. 661618 Ferdinand Figueroa
- C. 661818 Ferdnand Figueroa
- D. 661818 Ferdinand Figueroa

3. 100101 Norman D. Braustein   3.___

- A. 100101 Norman D. Braustein
- B. 101001 Norman D. Braustein
- C. 100101 Norman P. Braustien
- D. 100101 Norman D. Bruastein

4. 838696 Robert Kittredge   4.___

- A. 838969 Robert Kittredge
- B. 838696 Robert Kittredge
- C. 388696 Robert Kittredge
- D. 838696 Robert Kittridge

5. 243716 Abraham Soletsky   5.___

- A. 243716 Abrahm Soletsky
- B. 243716 Abraham Solestky
- C. 243176 Abraham Soletsky
- D. 243716 Abraham Soletsky

6. 981121 Phillip M. Maas   6.____

    A. 981121 Phillip M. Mass
    B. 981211 Phillip M. Maas
    C. 981121 Phillip M. Maas
    D. 981121 Phillip N. Maas

7. 786556 George Macalusso   7.____

    A. 785656 George Macalusso
    B. 786556 George Macalusso
    C. 786556 George Maculusso
    D. 786556 George Macluasso

8. 639472 Eugene Weber   8.____

    A. 639472 Eugene Weber
    B. 639472 Eugene Webre
    C. 693472 Eugene Weber
    D. 639742 Eugene Weber

9. 724936 John J. Lomonaco   9.____

    A. 724936 John J. Lomanoco
    B. 724396 John L. Lomonaco
    C. 724936 John J. Lomonaco
    D. 724936 John J. Lamonaco

10. 899868 Michael Schnitzer   10.____

    A. 899868 Micheal Schnitzer
    B. 898968 Michael Schnizter
    C. 899688 Michael Schnitzer
    D. 899868 Michael Schnitzer

KEY (CORRECT ANSWERS)

1.	C		6.	C
2.	D		7.	B
3.	A		8.	A
4.	B		9.	C
5.	D		10.	D

NAME AND NUMBER CHECKING

EXAMINATION SECTION
TEST 1

DIRECTIONS: This test is designed to measure your speed and accuracy. You are urged to work both quickly and accurately and to do correctly as many lists as you can in the time allowed. The test consists of lists of pairs of names and numbers. Count the number of IDENTICAL pairs in each list. Then, select the correct number, 1, 2, 3, 4, or 5, and indicate your choice by circling the corresponding number on your answer paper, Two sample questions are presented for your guidance, together with the correct solutions.

SAMPLE QUESTIONS

SAMPLE LIST A

		CIRCLE CORRECT ANSWER
Adelphi College	- Adelphia College	1 2 3 4 5
Braxton Corp.	- Braxeton Corp.	
Wassaic State School	- Wassaic State School	
Central Islip State Hospital	- Central Isllip State	
Greenwich House	- Greenwich House	

NOTE that there are only two correct pairs - Wassaic State School and Greenwich House. Therefore, the CORRECT answer is 2.

SAMPLE LIST B

78453694	- 78453684	1 2 3 4 5
784530	- 784530	
533	- 534	
67845	- 67845	
2368745	- 2368755	

NOTE that there are only two correct pairs - 784530 and 67845. Therefore, the CORRECT answer is 2.

LIST 1

98654327	- 98654327	1 2 3 4 5
74932564	- 74922564	
61438652	- 61438652	
01297653	- 01287653	
1865439765	- 1865439765	

LIST 2

478362	- 478363	1 2 3 4 5
278354792	- 278354772	
9327	- 9327	
297384625	- 27384625	
6428156	- 6428158	

LIST 3

Abbey House — Abbey House

1 2 3 4 5

Actors' Fund Home — Actor's Fund Home
Adrian Memorial — Adrian Memorial
A. Clayton Powell Home — Clayton Powell House
Abott E. Kittredge Club — Abbott E. Kitteredge Club

LIST 4

3682 — 3692   1 2 3 4 5
21937453829 — 31937453829
723 — 733
2763920 — 2763920
47293 — 47293

LIST 5

Adra House — Adra House   1 2 3 4 5
Adolescents' Court — Adolescents' Court
Cliff Villa — Cliff Villa
Clark Neighborhood House — Clark Neighborhood House
Alma Mathews House — Alma Mathews House

LIST 6

28734291 — 28734271   1 2 3 4 5
63810263849 — 63810263846
26831027 — 26831027
368291 — 368291
7238102637 — 7238102637

LIST 7

Albion State T.S. — Albion State T.C.   1 2 3 4 5
Clara de Hirsch Home — Clara De Hirsch Home
Alice Carrington Royce — Alice Carington Royce
Alice Chopin Nursery — Alice Chapin Nursery
Lighthouse Eye Clinic — Lighthouse Eye Clinic

LIST 8

327 — 329   1 2 3 4 5
712438291026 — 712438291026
2753829142 — 275382942
826287 — 826289
26435162839 — 26435162839

LIST 9

Letchworth Village — Letchworth Village   1 2 3 4 5
A.A.A.E. Inc. — A.A.A.E. Inc.
Clear Pool Camp — Clear Pool Camp
A.M.M.L.A. Inc. — A.M.M.L.A. Inc.
J.G. Harbard — J.G. Harbord

LIST 10
8254	- 8256	1 2 3 4 5
2641526	- 2641526	
4126389012	- 4126389102	
725	- 725	
76253917287	- 76253917287	

LIST 11
Attica State Prison	- Attica State Prison	1 2 3 4 5
Nellie Murrah	- Nellie Murrah	
Club Marshall	- Club Marshal	
Assissium Casea-Maria	- Assissium Casa-Maria	
The Homestead	- The Homestead	

LIST 12
2691	- 2691	1 2 3 4 5
623819253627	- 623819253629	
28637	- 28937	
278392736	- 278392736	
52739	- 52739	

LIST 13
A.I.C.P. Boys Camp	- A.I.C.P. Boy's Camp	1 2 3 4 5
Einar Chrystie	- Einar Christyie	
Astoria Center	- Astoria Center	
G. Frederick Brown	- G. Federick Browne	
Vacation Service	- Vacation Services	

LIST 14
728352689	- 728352688	1 2 3 4 5
643728	- 643728	
37829176	- 37827196	
8425367	- 8425369	
65382018	- 65382018	

LIST 15
E.S. Streim	- E.S. Strim	1 2 3 4 5
Charles E. Higgins	- Charles E. Higgins	
Baluvelt, N.Y.	- Blauwelt, N.Y.	
Roberta Magdalen	- Roberto Magdalen	
Ballard School	- Ballard School	

LIST 16
7382	- 7392	1 2 3 4 5
281374538299	- 291374538299	
623	- 633	
6273730	- 6273730	
63392	- 63392	

LIST 17
Orrin Otis — - Orrin Otis   1 2 3 4 5
Barat Settlement — - Barat Settlemen
Emmanuel House — - Emmanuel House
William T. McCreery - William T. McCreery
Seamen's Home — - Seaman's Home

LIST 18
72824391 — - 72834371   1 2 3 4 5
3729106237 — - 37291106237
82620163849 — - 82620163846
37638921 — - 37638921
82631027 — - 82631027

LIST 19
Commonwealth Fund — - Commonwealth Fund   1 2 3 4 5
Anne Johnsen — - Anne Johnson
Bide-a-Wee Home — - Bide-a-Wee Home
Riverdale-on-Hudson — - Riverdal-on-Hudson
Bialystoker Home — - Bailystoker Home

LIST 20
9271 — - 9271   1 2 3 4 5
392918352627 — - 392018852629
72637 — - 72637
927392736 — - 927392736
92739 — - 92739

LIST 21
Charles M. Stump — - Charles M. Stump   1 2 3 4 5
Bourne Workshop — - Buorne Workshop
B'nai Bi'rith — - B'nai Brith
Poppenhuesen Institute — - Poppenheusen Institute
Consular Service — - Consular Service

LIST 22
927352689 — - 927352688   1 2 3 4 5
647382 — - 648382
93729176 — - 93727196
649536718 — - 649536718
5835367 — - 5835369

LIST 23
L.S. Bestend — - L.S. Bestent   1 2 3 4 5
Hirsch Mfg. Co. — - Hircsh Mfg. Co.
F.H. Storrs — - F.P. Storrs
Camp Wassaic — - Camp Wassaic
George Ballingham - George Ballingham

126

LIST 24

372846392048	- 372846392048
334	- 334
7283524678	- 7283524678
7283	- 7283
7283629372	- 7283629372

CIRCLE
CORRECT ANSWER
1 2 3 4 5

LIST 25

Dr. Stiles Company	- Dr. Stills Company
Frances Hunsdon	- Frances Hunsdon
Northrop Barrert	- Nothrup Barrent
J. D. Brunjes	- J. D. Brunjes
Theo. Claudel & Co.	- Theo. Claudel co.

1 2 3 4 5

———

KEY (CORRECT ANSWERS)

1.	3	11.	3
2.	1	12.	3
3.	2	13.	1
4.	2	14.	2
5.	5	15.	2
6.	3	16.	2
7.	1	17.	3
8.	2	18.	2
9.	4	19.	2
10.	3	20.	4

21.	2
22.	1
23.	2
24.	5
25.	2

———

TEST 2

DIRECTIONS: This test is designed to measure your speed and accuracy. You are urged to work both quickly and accurately and to do correctly as many lists as you can in the time allowed. The test consists of lists of pairs of names and numbers. Count the number of IDENTICAL pairs in each list. Then, select the correct number, 1, 2, 3, 4, or 5, and indicate your choice by circling the corresponding number on your answer paper, Two sample questions are presented for your guidance, together with the correct solutions.

LIST 1

82728	- 82738	CIRCLE
82736292637	- 82736292639	CORRECT ANSWER
728	- 738	1 2 3 4 5
83926192527	- 83726192529	
82736272	- 82736272	

LIST 2

L. Pietri	- L. Pietri	
Mathewson, L.F.	- Mathewson, L.F.	
Funk & Wagnall	- Funk &. Wagnalls	1 2 3 4 5
Shimizu, Sojio	- Shimizu, Sojio	
Filing Equipment Bureau	- Filing Equipment Buraeu	

LIST 3

63801829374	- 63801839474	
283577657	- 283577657	
65689	- 65689	1 2 3 4 5
3457892026	- 3547893026	
2779	- 2778	

LIST 4

August Caille	- August Caille	
The Well-Fare Service	- The Wel-Fare Service	
K.L.M. Process Co.	- R.L.M. Process Co.	1 2 3 4 5
Merrill Littell	- Merrill Littell	
Dodd & Sons	- Dodd & Son	

LIST 5

998745732	- 998745733	
723	- 723	
463849102983	- 463849102983	1 2 3 4 5
8570	- 8570	
279012	- 279012	

LIST 6

M. A. Wender	- M.A. Winder	
Minneapolis Supply Co.	- Minneapolis Supply Co.	
Beverly Hills Corp	- Beverley Hills Corp.	1 2 3 4 5
Trafalgar Square	- Trafalgar Square	
Phifer, D.T.	- Phiefer, D.T.	

CIRCLE
CORRECT ANSWER

LIST 7
7834629	- 7834629
3549806746	- 3549806746
97802564	- 97892564
689246	- 688246
2578024683	- 2578024683

1 2 3 4 5

LIST 8
Scadrons'	- Scadrons'
Gensen & Bro.	- Genson & Bro.
Firestone Co.	- Firestone Co.
H.L. Eklund	- H.L. Eklund
Oleomargarine Co.	- Oleomargarine Co.

1 2 3 4 5

LIST 9
782039485618	- 782039485618
53829172639	- 63829172639
892	- 892
82937482	- 829374820
52937456	- 53937456

1 2 3 4 5

LIST 10
First Nat'l Bank	- First Nat'l Bank
Sedgwick Machine Works	- Sedgewick Machine Works
Hectographia Co.	- Hectographia Corp.
Levet Bros.	- Levet Bros.
Multistamp Co.,Inc.	- Multistamp Co.,Inc.

1 2 3 4 5

LIST 11
7293	- 7293
6382910293	- 6382910292
981928374012	- 981928374912
58293	- 58393
18203649271	- 283019283745

1 2 3 4 5

LIST 12
Lowrey Lb'r Co.	- Lowrey Lb'r Co.
Fidelity Service	- Fidelity Service
Reumann, J.A.	- Reumann, J.A.
Duophoto Ltd.	- Duophotos Ltd.
John Jarratt	- John Jaratt

1 2 3 4 5

LIST 13
6820384	- 6820384
383019283745	- 383019283745
63927102	- 63928102
91029354829	- 91029354829
58291728	- 58291728

1 2 3 4 5

LIST 14
Standard Press Co.	- Standard Press Co.
Reliant Mf'g. Co.	- Relant Mf'g Co.
M.C. Lynn	- M.C. Lynn
J. Fredericks Company	- G. Fredericks Company
Wandermann, B.S.	- Wanderman, B.S.

1 2 3 4 5

LIST 15
4283910293	- 4283010203
992018273648	- 992018273848
620	- 629
752937273	- 752937373
5392	- 5392

1 2 3 4 5

LIST 16
Waldorf Hotel	- Waldorf Hotel
Aaron Machinery Co.	- Aaron Machinery Co.
Caroline Ann Locke	- Caroline Anne Locke
McCabe Mfg. Co.	- McCabe Mfg. Co.
R.L. Landres	- R.L. Landers

1 2 3 4 5

LIST 17
68391028364	- 68391028394
68293	- 68293
739201	- 739201
72839201	- 72839211
739917	- 739719

1 2 3 4 5

LIST 18
Balsam M.M.	- Balsamm, M.M.
Steinway & Co.	- Stienway & M. Co.
Eugene Elliott	- Eugene A. Elliott
Leonard Loan Co.	- Leonard Loan Co.
Frederick Morgan	- Frederick Morgen

1 2 3 4 5

LIST 19
8929	- 9820
392836472829	- 392836472829
462	- 462 2039271
827	- 2039276837
53829	- 54829

1 2 3 4 5

LIST 20
Danielson's Hofbrau	- Danielson's Hafbrau
Edward A. Truarme	- Edward A. Truame
Insulite Co.	- Insulite Co.
Reisler Shoe Corp,	- Rielser Shoe Corp.
L.L. Thompson	- L.L. Thompson

1 2 3 4 5

LIST 21

		1 2 3 4 5
92839102837	- 92839102837	
58891028	- 58891028	
7291728	- 7291928	
272839102839	- 272839102839	
428192	- 428102	

LIST 22

		1 2 3 4 5
K.L. Veiller	- K.L. Veiller	
Webster, Roy	- Webster, Ray	
Drasner Spring Co.	- Drasner Spring Co.	
Edward J. Cravenport	- Edward J. Cravanport	
Harold Field	- Harold A. Field	

LIST 23

		1 2 3 4 5
2293	- 2293	
4283910293	- 5382910292	
871928374012	- 871928374912	
68293	- 68393	
8120364927	- 81293649271	

LIST 24

		1 2 3 4 5
Tappe, Inc	- Tappe, Inc.	
A.M. Wentingworth	- A.M. Wentinworth	
Scott A. Elliott	- Scott A. Elliott	
Echeverria Corp.	- Echeverria Corp.	
Bradford Victor Company	- Bradford Victer Company	

LIST 25

		1 2 3 4 5
4820384	- 4820384	
393019283745	- 283919283745	
63927102	- 63927102	
91029354829	- 91029354829	
48291728	- 48291728	

KEY (CORRECT ANSWERS)

1.	1		11.	1
2.	3		12.	3
3.	2		13.	4
4.	2		14.	2
5.	4		15.	1
6.	2		16.	3
7.	3		17.	2
8.	4		18.	1
9.	2		19.	1
10.	3		20.	2

21.	3
22.	2
23.	1
24.	2
25.	4

———